I0521139

# D1 OFFERS

## STUDENT-ATHLETE & PARENTS' GUIDE
## TO AN ATHLETIC SCHOLARSHIP

## MICHAEL A. WATERS

D1 OFFERS

Student-Athlete & Parents' Guide to an Athletic Scholarship

Copyright © 2025. Michael Waters. All rights reserved. No part of this publication may be reproduced, distributed, or transmitted in any form or by any means, including photocopying, recording, or other electronic or mechanical methods, without the prior written permission of the publisher, except in the case of brief quotations embodied in critical reviews and certain other noncommercial uses permitted by copyright law.

If you'd like to bring the strategies of *D1 Offers* to your school, team, or organization, I am available for speaking engagements nationwide. Whether it's a parent night, athlete workshop, or coach training session, I tailor each presentation to empower and educate.

Bulk book orders are also available for programs, events, or team distributions.

For bookings and bulk pricing, please contact me directly at mwaters@phase1sports.com.

Phase 1 Sports, Inc.
2015 E. Windmill Lane
Las Vegas, NV 89123
www.phase1sports.com

ISBN: 979-8-9931662-4-7

Book Design by Transcendent Publishing
Editing by Mary Rembert

The author makes no guarantees regarding the level of success readers may achieve by following the advice and strategies outlined in this book. Individual results will vary, and readers accept the inherent risks that outcomes may differ. Testimonials and examples provided represent exceptional results and are not intended to guarantee or suggest that similar results will be achieved.

*"Opportunities don't happen. You create them."*

–Chris Grosser

# DEDICATION

To everyone who has been part of the Phase 1 Sports Family over the past 20 years—athletes, families, coaches, and supporters—this book is for you. I'll forever be grateful for your belief, dedication, and commitment that continue to impact lives and open doors for our youth. Thank you for being part of the mission.

# TABLE OF CONTENTS

# THE POWER OF A FULL-RIDE SCHOLARSHIP

For some athletes, a full-ride scholarship may be the only means of going to college. For others, it can be a lifetime dream of playing at the next level and getting it all paid for. Still others may get a late start, but quickly realize they have a natural gift that allows them to dominate their sport.

In either case, receiving a full ride is an accomplishment that not many people can say they achieved. To say that it is competitive is an understatement.

Let's discuss a full-ride scholarship by the numbers. First of all, let's be clear, full-ride scholarships are relatively rare. Most universities have limited funds and scholarship budgets. Not to mention that the NCAA also regulates the number of scholarships that are available to control the competitive advantage from college to college. We also have to factor in the most recent NCAA changes to roster limitations, scholarships, and NIL opportunities.

There are a few factors to consider, so let's start at the top of the scholarship food chain with NCAA Division I programs. Did you know that only about 2% of high school athletes receive any form of athletic scholarship to compete in college?

To make the odds even more challenging, full-ride scholarships are typically only offered in a few sports. FBS Football programs, for example, currently have 85 full scholarships available, while basketball has 13. There are four women's sports that offer full-ride scholarships: basketball, with 15 available; tennis, which has eight full scholarships; and volleyball and gymnastics, both of which have 12 full scholarships available.

These are the "headcount" sports, meaning the number of scholarships is directly related to a specific number of athletes. Most other sports (e.g., baseball, soccer, track & field, swimming, golf, and softball) are equivalency sports. Coaches get a set number of scholarship dollars and can split them among athletes. Full rides are possible, but not guaranteed—they are usually reserved for elite athletes who can cover multiple event needs or roster roles.

But don't worry, that is why you are here. This book will be your golden ticket to accomplishing the goal of a full-ride scholarship. When I started Phase 1 Sports in 2003, I had one simple goal. It was a very big goal, but a simple one. I wanted to help high school athletes get scholarships.

My experience going through the recruiting process in high school and again after graduating from junior college was the perfect learning ground for what I do today. We have all heard that everything happens for a reason, and this is one of those times that I can connect the dots.

In my senior year of high school, I had multiple scholarship offers, but did not qualify academically. I attended a junior college and, after two seasons, was able to transfer to UNLV, a Division I school.

The reason I share that is because my story is the actual reason I started Phase 1 Sports. My family and I had never gone through the recruiting process, and to be transparent, I was the first in my family to attend college.

I remember having a conversation with my mother about wanting to go to college to play football. She was excited, and she believed that I could accomplish that goal. However, she made it clear that she had no idea how to help make that happen.

That led me to realize very quickly that I had to figure this out on my own. As my days as a college athlete were coming to an end, I started to think about what career path I would take. Would I search for a marketing job on the Strip in Las Vegas at one of the major hotels, or would I start a marketing company and work with businesses? These were all thoughts that I had at the time.

But the more I thought about it, the more I wanted to stay close to what I loved the most. Sports. There were sports agents, sports marketing, or working in the front office of a sports team, but none of those interested me.

After a few months of brainstorming, I looked at the role that football had played in my life, how my college experience exposed me to so many different things: traveling, friendships, spring break parties, and everything in between.

Then I started thinking about my recruiting experience and how I was lucky to accomplish my goal of playing Division I football, but it came so close to not happening. After not qualifying academically out of high school, I literally decided that I was done with football. The disappointment was too much to deal with at the time.

Without going into too much detail, I was lost and going down the wrong path. I woke up about 12 months later and realized that I really missed football. Not school, just football, so I decided to make a comeback.

Very shortly after that decision, I was back in the weight room, training on my own, and I enrolled at Mt. San Antonio College, where I was back on the field.

Two years later, I was putting on a Division I helmet at the University of Nevada, Las Vegas. After two years at UNLV, it was time to hang the helmet up for the last time.

You may be thinking, Why not the NFL? To make a long story short, I did not produce the statistics in college to have the opportunity to play at the highest level. Instead of chasing a dream that was not within reach, I pursued my passion and founded Phase 1 Sports.

Since then, we have successfully helped 800+ athletes by using the same strategies that you will be learning in the upcoming chapters. This is a great time to get your pen and paper ready and take some notes. My goal is to provide you with tangible steps and strategies that you can implement immediately. So let's get into it.

Have you thought about the impact that a full-ride scholarship will have on your future? Accomplishing this goal will put you into an elite group of athletes. Less than 2% of the athlete community, to be exact, so that leads me to a question. Are you willing and ready to do what it takes to accomplish your goal of getting that full-ride scholarship?

Before you read any further, you should answer that question. As a parent, the question is very similar: Are you willing to provide your child with the resources to accomplish this goal? If the answer is yes, let's get into the information that will help you secure a full-ride scholarship.

One of the first things that comes to mind is the financial relief that a scholarship provides. A full-ride scholarship covers tuition, room and board, books, and, in most cases, other additional expenses.

Imagine attending a Division I athletic program and having everything paid for. This can save families thousands of dollars per year. Even if you have a college fund, a full ride can free up money for other opportunities.

Not to mention that a full ride will also reduce, if not eliminate, the need for student loans, and we all know how bad those can be over a four- to six-year period.

For parents, this is always a great conversation. It's your responsibility to provide the resources for your children, and what better way to send your student-athlete off to college than on a full-ride scholarship that will provide them with access to high-quality education, advanced facilities, and a broader network of opportunities for future careers.

This book is not about becoming a professional athlete, although that is a possibility. This book was written to focus 100% on becoming a college student-athlete. So, let's discuss how a full-ride scholarship can remove additional stress and workload, allowing athletes to focus more on academics, training, and personal growth.

When an athlete is on a full-ride scholarship, the university requires very high academic and athletic standards. The majority of your time will be occupied with classes, workouts, practices, and travel. Being a college student-athlete is a commitment that should not be taken lightly. It is a full-time job, and now that NIL (Name, Image, Likeness) has been approved, it's a job that pays very well. Or at least it *can* pay very well.

To maintain these standards, the NCAA even restricts how many hours you can work a part-time job. Some athletes may not like the control the NCAA has over student-athletes, but being on a full ride does reduce the amount of money needed for day-to-day expenses.

That is the trade-off and the partnership between you, the student-athlete, and the university. On June 30, 2021, the NCAA approved its interim name, image, and likeness policy. That policy has changed the financial landscape of college sports forever. In a later chapter, I will go into detail about NIL and how to capitalize on the new policy.

As if tuition, room, and board being paid is not enough, let's talk more about the perks of being a college athlete. These should bring a smile to your face because being a college athlete literally changes the college experience.

Don't get me wrong, being a college student-athlete has its downsides. It can make you feel like you have no freedom to do the things that other nonathlete students can do. You may find yourself battling between your social life and your commitment to your sport. It can be a battle, and, in my experience, the athletes who struggle the most are the ones who try to balance both worlds.

You must be committed to your goal of being a college athlete, not just to get a scholarship, but to actually compete and contribute to the team, and to keep your scholarship. I've seen a number of athletes get to college and totally lose focus. They get caught up in the social life, party life, alcohol, drugs, and before they realize it, they are completely derailed.

For some athletes, it's the first time they experience freedom. No mom, no dad, just their discipline versus the peer pressure that comes with the college environment. This means that you have to be locked in and focused on day 1 if you plan on being a successful college athlete.

Being a college student-athlete is on a whole other level. For example, the boosters. Yes, boosters, because I don't have a better word for them. The boosters are committed to the team's success and are willing to put financial resources behind it. They are typically alumni and business owners, and many are very wealthy and very invested in the sports programs.

In the new NIL era, the boosters have joined forces to create what is now being called "collectives." What's a collective? To keep it simple, a collective is a group of boosters, businesses, etc., that pool their money together and use the revenue to pay student-athletes who attend or are committed to attending their school of interest.

For example, a 5-Star athlete may be enticed to commit to a university after being offered hundreds of thousands and even millions of dollars. You can imagine how powerful these groups can become and how they can completely disrupt college sports, which we are already seeing happen.

To be clear, this is reserved for the 4- and 5-Star athletes in the world, but all athletes can now participate in Name, Image, and Likeness revenue, which is why I will be discussing the importance of building your brand in a later chapter.

Throughout your time as an athlete, you should focus on building relationships with collectives, individual boosters, and alumni. Not just for the perks while you are a student, but for the relationship that can give you an advantage after graduation.

Like I tell my athletes, even if you make it to the pros, you'll spend more years in the "real world" than you spend as a pro athlete. That alone is a great reason to start building relationships sooner rather than later.

While playing football at UNLV, I was able to make some lifelong connections, including one with the co-owner of the Las Vegas Athletic Clubs. LVAC is basically comparable to the national chain 24 Hour Fitness. In Las Vegas, it is one of the largest commercial gyms in the state. There are multiple locations and thousands of members.

During the summer, I worked there to earn a couple of extra dollars. While working there, the co-owner took a liking to me. From day one, it was like I was his favorite employee. Looking back, it was simple; he gave me preferential treatment just because I was a football player at UNLV.

He would call me into his office just to talk sports. He wanted to talk about the season goals, the games, the practices, and everything else related to the team. It was like I was his personal reporter, giving him the inside scoop. We ate lunch together a couple of times, and over time, we built a pretty good relationship.

What does that have to do with getting a scholarship? Nothing at all. But it has everything to do with the benefits and perks of being a college athlete. Once my football career ended, I started my business working with student-athletes.

After the first two years in business, I realized that my athletes needed more than just help with recruiting. They needed to become athletes who were complete in every area. They needed to be bigger, faster, stronger, and more athletic if they were going to get the attention of college coaches.

That led me to start Phase 1 Sports Performance Training, and one year later, I opened my first Athlete Performance Training Center. Pretty ironic, yes, I would say so. During the time I was working at LVAC, owning my own facility was not one of my goals. However, I had learned so much from my experience working there and my relationship with the owner that I was confident that it would be successful.

Over the next few years, we expanded from one location to multiple locations in Las Vegas and one in Hawaii.

Here's what is cool about that experience: when you are going through your college years, you can't always see how beneficial a relationship will be in the future. So I always advise my athletes to keep in contact with as many people as possible along the way.

You'll be surprised how years later a connection can get you an oppor-tunity or a great referral that can change your life. So keep your eyes open for opportunities. Take advantage of exclusive networking events, career resources, and mentorships, which can all help build a foundation for your career beyond sports.

I say this to say, don't wait until you graduate to start building your professional network. I wrote this chapter to give you a different per-spective on how playing at the college level can be life-changing. Now, let's get into the reason you started reading this book.

## KEY POINTS:

- D1 schools have the largest athletic budgets and the highest competition levels.
- Not all sports offer full scholarships; many are partial.
- Athletic and academic performance are both critical.

# CHAPTER 1

# UNDERSTANDING THE SCHOLARSHIP LANDSCAPE

Many families have a misconception about what it takes to get a full-ride scholarship. Some believe that if you are good, college coaches will find you. Others believe that all it takes is your high school coach promoting you to colleges. Some don't have a clue, and they trust in recruiting services like NCSA.

These thoughts are all normal and typical of families that are going through the recruiting process for the first time. Before I go into detail on the scholarship landscape, let me touch on each of these topics.

There was a time when college coaches spent all their energy and time searching for athletes to recruit. They would travel from state to state, city to city, big schools, small schools, and everything in between. They took pride in recruiting nationally ranked athletes and even more pride in finding the under-the-radar talent across the country.

College coaches evaluated based on athleticism, skill, and overall potential. They would then bring athletes into the program, spend a year or two in development, and the next thing you know, the athlete becomes one of the best in the country.

I'm not saying that coaches are not recruiting the same way, but I am saying times have changed. The demand for winning is very high for college coaches today, so they have to spend more time on game plans, preparation, and making sure athletes are game-ready.

On average, college coaches are working 12 to 16 hours a day, six days a week, sometimes seven. The turnover in college coaching is as high as it has ever been. It's a business, and winning is the only sure way to keep your job.

With these new demands, coaches have become more reliant on national scouting services that evaluate talent and create national rankings. Some of the major services include 247 Sports, Rivals, and ESPNU, to name a few. These services claim to provide an unbiased evaluation of athletes nationwide.

The reason I say they claim to provide an unbiased evaluation is that politics will always play a role in the recruiting process. That doesn't mean that these services are not valuable. We have great relationships with regional and national scouts for the major scouting groups. They have been very valuable in assisting our athletes in gaining exposure. Later in this book, we will discuss more about these services and how to make sure you are ranked.

To be clear, scouting services are very different from recruiting services like NCSA. Recruiting services claim to help athletes get scholarships by providing paid recruiting assistance. Here is why I'm not a big fan of these types of services, based on my 20+ years of experience.

Number one, they typically have tens of thousands of athletes in their database. That's great for business and generating revenue for the recruiting service, but not so great for individual athletes. This also means that there are thousands of similar athletes in the database, hoping to get the attention of college coaches.

From the initial conversation, the concept makes sense: create a profile with all of your information and wait for college coaches to find you. While waiting, you can also send college coaches messages. It sounds like a great plan until you realize that not many coaches actually use the service.

But what about the testimonials and the families that have successfully used these services? My answer is simple: it's a numbers game. If there are thousands of athletes paying for this service, there will be some success stories. But the question is, did they get that result from the recruiting service or by being a good athlete?

Here's what I have found to be true when it comes to recruiting services. College coaches know that parents have paid for this service, and therefore, they don't value the database as much as the recruiting services will try to convince you.

These services also do not evaluate or rank athletes on a national scale, so it makes it very difficult for college coaches to determine which athletes to recruit out of the thousands of profiles.

I've also made it a point to ask a number of Division I and Division II college coaches if they utilize these services to recruit, and I've not received one yes. In the sales pitch, they will promote the fact that every college coach has access to their database, and that may be true. But access does not guarantee that college coaches are logging in and actually evaluating and recruiting athletes.

As you can see, my opinion on this is very strong, and here is why. Over the years, I have had so many athletes come to me for help after two to three years of being in a recruiting service. After spending thousands of dollars, at the end of the recruiting journey, there's nothing.

To be fair, there is one case where a recruiting service may be beneficial, and that is if you are seeking to play at the Division III or NAIA level. I say this because I have heard of lower-level college coaches searching these websites to initiate the recruiting process. College programs in the lower divisions often lack the recruiting budget to travel the country, so there is some benefit to them to search for athletes who may be a good fit for their program. But, even then, I don't see the value in something you can do for yourself.

Not to be a complete hater, there is one thing that I love about some of the recruiting services out there. The advanced websites feature super-detailed athlete profiles that track college coach contacts and links to track views and visits, which are all great. College coaches can search for athletes based on region, statistics, etc., which is super cool if a college coach is actually on the platform searching.

So don't feel bad if you have already invested in one of these services. As a parent, it's all about doing the best you can to ensure your student-athlete has a chance, and that's what you were doing.

Now is a good time to thank the person who led you to this book. My job is to equip you with the tools and strategies to launch a successful recruiting campaign without spending thousands of dollars.

Before we get into the logistics of getting a full-ride scholarship, let's build a foundational understanding of what is available.

NCAA Division I offers the most available full-ride scholarships. These full rides are most common in football (FBS), men's and women's basketball, women's volleyball, women's gymnastics, and tennis. The correlation is simple: these are the sports that generate the majority of the revenue for college institutions and the NCAA. Division I football FBS (Football Bowl Subdivision) leads the way, generating $5-6 billion per year in revenue.

For these sports, the scholarship must cover full tuition, room, board, and books. This is why these are also the most competitive sports, where about 2% of eligible athletes receive full-ride scholarships.

If that is your goal, having a solid understanding of what is available will be key. To be in that 2%, it is going to take some work, not just on the field or court, but off the field as well. Keep in mind that you are competing with thousands of athletes around the country, not just the athletes in your area.

NCAA Division II full-ride scholarships are very limited. It is not impossible to receive one, but they are limited. D2 scholarships are usually partial, meaning they will pay for a portion of a student-athlete's expenses.

Once the amount is determined, these institutions will work on grants, academic scholarships, etc., to further assist financially. As an athlete or the parent of an athlete, the goal should be very simple. Get school paid for!

During the recruiting process, college coaches will typically communicate the type of scholarship that is available and exactly what will be offered. To be clear, this does not mean that a student-athlete is not eligible to apply for additional scholarships, financial aid, and other grants. In most cases, the college coach will work to get you to a "full ride." I know what you're thinking, "You said D2 schools don't often offer full rides." Let me explain my definition of a full ride. When an offer letter is received, there is a section at the very bottom that states something along the lines of Parent/Family financial responsibility. That section will determine how much the family is responsible for in order for you to attend that university.

As I mentioned earlier and want to mention again, as an athlete and a parent, you should only have one goal. That goal should be to get your college education paid for. So, if the bottom of that offer letter says $0, guess what? You are on a full ride.

Don't concern yourself with how a college puts the offer together; be more concerned about having all of your expenses paid for. That can be athletic, academic, grants, other scholarships, in-state tuition, or a number of other options. The goal is to get a free education and play the sport you love at the college level.

NCAA Division III colleges do not offer athletic scholarships at all. Instead, student-athletes may receive academic scholarships, grants, or other financial aid, but they are not based on athletic ability.

This is why it is very important that high school student-athletes focus on academic excellence. This will increase the chances of getting your college education paid for. This should not discourage you by any means. Similar to Division II colleges, it's all about getting your education paid for. However, the main focus of D3 programs is on your academic performance. That will be the difference between getting recruited or not.

Before a college coach gets too deep into the recruiting process, they will request transcripts and test scores to determine your academic qualifications. This will give them the blueprint on what type of financial package they can create for you.

NAIA is the National Association of Intercollegiate Athletics. The NAIA colleges offer both full-ride and partial scholarships; however, the majority are partial. This means you will again have to rely upon academic scholarships and other grants.

As you can see, there is one thing that is consistent—academics. Your production in your sport is obviously a significant factor in your potential college choice. However, I will tell you from experience, it's the academics that separate you from your competition.

So, what is the overall goal? During my consultations with student-athletes and their families, I always ask this question. The answer helps me determine if I want to take on this family as a client. I'm sure you're wondering what the right answer is to the question.

Let me start with what the wrong answer is: "I want to get a D1 full-ride scholarship." Confused? Isn't that the goal?

Actually, it's not the goal. The goal is to get your college education paid for! My goal for every athlete that I work with is the same. At the bottom of your offer letter, I want to see $0. That means that you are on a full ride. It may be all athletic, a combination of athletic and academic, or it could be all academic. But at the end of the day, the goal is to get your college education paid for.

Let me be clear: I want every athlete I work with to go D1. However, we must be realistic in knowing that not every athlete is a D1 athlete, so we don't want to limit the opportunity to play at the next level. That is a mistake I often see from athletes and their families. The focus is on Division I, and they are not open to other opportunities, or they never pursue other options. We do produce dozens of D1 scholarships per year, but that is still just a small percentage of athletes in our program.

To increase your opportunities, you want to be open to every level of competition. The cool thing is that over time, as you launch your recruiting campaign, the responses from college coaches will help you determine your personal potential.

My professional advice would be to adopt all of the habits of a Division I athlete. Focus on training and making sure that you are in great shape, strong, explosive, and continuing to develop athletically. Lock in on the nutrition and supplements that will be beneficial for your personal physical goals. Continue to improve and develop the skills that will assure you are dominant in your sport.

Most importantly, make academic success your number one priority. Think of your academics as the tiebreaker. If a college coach has narrowed it down to two athletes who are very similar in skill and athletic ability, but that coach can only offer a scholarship to one of them, what is the tiebreaker they will use to decide? I can tell you right now that it will likely come down to academics. So as you progress through your high school career, continue to develop, to get better, and to work toward your goal of being a D1 athlete.

# CHAPTER 2

# NAVIGATING THE ACADEMIC AND ATHLETIC ROAD TO A SCHOLARSHIP

In this chapter, I will outline a year-by-year strategy starting in your freshman year. I'm fully aware that you may already be a sophomore, junior, or possibly even a senior. In that case, I would still ask that you go through each year to ensure you have been taking the proper steps.

Even if you feel like you are behind, it's better to know than to find out when it's too late. What's also cool is that you can complete most of the steps if you haven't already. So if you are an upperclassman, don't worry. Worst-case scenario, you may have a little extra work to do, but it will be worth it.

## GETTING STARTED WITH FRESHMAN YEAR

In your freshman year, you need to establish a strong academic foundation. Aim for strong grades from the start; colleges will want to see transcripts for all four years of high school.

Starting in your freshman year, you should be focusing on core courses like math, science, English, and social studies. Here is why this is so important. To be eligible for an athletic scholarship, the NCAA requires student-athletes to complete a specific number of core courses by graduation.

Let's start with NCAA Division I institutions and what is required for an athletic scholarship. My job is to make this very simple to understand; however, for more clarification on academic requirements, please visit the NCAA website.

For NCAA Division I colleges, 16 core courses are required: four years of English, three years of math, which must include algebra one or higher, and two years of natural or physical science, including one year of lab science if it is offered at your school.

You will also need one additional year of English, math, or science, two years of social science, and four additional years of any of the above or a foreign language, philosophy, or comparative religion.

The following graphic includes NCAA Division I and Division II requirements. Division III and NAIA schools set their own academic standards.

You can see why starting with a strong academic foundation in your freshman year is so important. To get a head start and set the tempo, I would schedule a meeting with an academic counselor at the start of your freshman year. That way, they know from the start that your goal is to be eligible for a D1 athletic scholarship. This will help with creating your class schedule and four-year worksheet for eligibility.

If you are an upperclassman, now is a good time to schedule a meeting with your academic counselor to ensure that you are on track academically. The sooner the better, so that you have time to make adjustments, retake classes, and add additional summer school classes if needed. Meeting these core course requirements is essential for NCAA eligibility.

Student-athletes should also register with the NCAA Eligibility Center to ensure they are meeting all necessary academic standards for

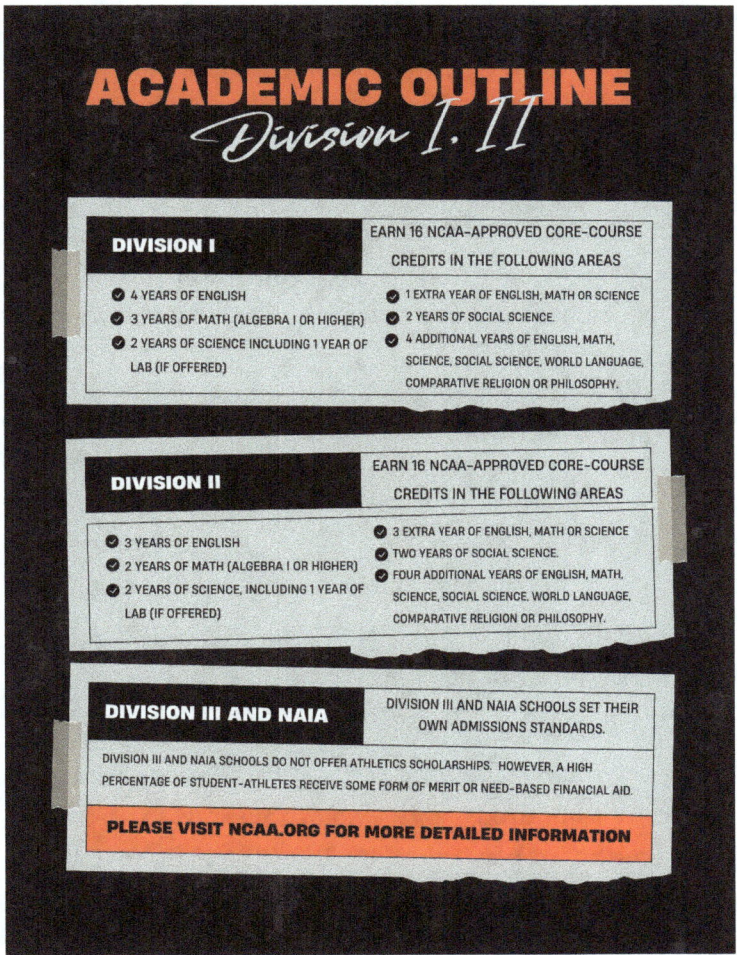

**ACADEMIC OUTLINE**
*Division* I. II

| DIVISION I | EARN 16 NCAA-APPROVED CORE-COURSE CREDITS IN THE FOLLOWING AREAS |
|---|---|
| ✓ 4 YEARS OF ENGLISH<br>✓ 3 YEARS OF MATH (ALGEBRA I OR HIGHER)<br>✓ 2 YEARS OF SCIENCE INCLUDING 1 YEAR OF LAB (IF OFFERED) | ✓ 1 EXTRA YEAR OF ENGLISH, MATH OR SCIENCE<br>✓ 2 YEARS OF SOCIAL SCIENCE.<br>✓ 4 ADDITIONAL YEARS OF ENGLISH, MATH, SCIENCE, SOCIAL SCIENCE, WORLD LANGUAGE, COMPARATIVE RELIGION OR PHILOSOPHY. |

| DIVISION II | EARN 16 NCAA-APPROVED CORE-COURSE CREDITS IN THE FOLLOWING AREAS |
|---|---|
| ✓ 3 YEARS OF ENGLISH<br>✓ 2 YEARS OF MATH (ALGEBRA I OR HIGHER)<br>✓ 2 YEARS OF SCIENCE, INCLUDING 1 YEAR OF LAB (IF OFFERED) | ✓ 3 EXTRA YEAR OF ENGLISH, MATH OR SCIENCE<br>✓ TWO YEARS OF SOCIAL SCIENCE.<br>✓ FOUR ADDITIONAL YEARS OF ENGLISH, MATH, SCIENCE, SOCIAL SCIENCE, WORLD LANGUAGE, COMPARATIVE RELIGION OR PHILOSOPHY. |

| DIVISION III AND NAIA | DIVISION III AND NAIA SCHOOLS SET THEIR OWN ADMISSIONS STANDARDS. |
|---|---|

DIVISION III AND NAIA SCHOOLS DO NOT OFFER ATHLETICS SCHOLARSHIPS. HOWEVER, A HIGH PERCENTAGE OF STUDENT-ATHLETES RECEIVE SOME FORM OF MERIT OR NEED-BASED FINANCIAL AID.

**PLEASE VISIT NCAA.ORG FOR MORE DETAILED INFORMATION**

athletic scholarships. The eligibility center will look at the progression of your high school academics by year and determine if you are on track and trending toward completing all academic core classes and requirements. This is the initial screening that college coaches use to determine if you are on track academically.

Athletically, in your freshman year, you should focus on skill development and training specific to your sport. Along with competing at the high school level, you should be competing on club or travel teams for more exposure and a wider array of competition. This is also a great time to begin attending camps or clinics, if possible.

Your main focus is to develop your skills and gain as much feedback as possible from coaches. This is a work year, not an evaluation year.

Here's what I mean. As a freshman, you are three to four years out from heading off to college. You have time before you need to start comparing yourself to older athletes and deciding what level you can compete at in college.

Instead, focus 100% on getting better and maximizing your first year of high school. If you are comparing yourself to upperclassmen, do it only to determine what areas you may need to develop. There is so much growth that will happen between your freshman and senior year, so there's no need to compare; only a need to work and get better.

## MOVING ON TO YOUR SOPHOMORE YEAR

In your sophomore year, you must maintain academic progress. Academics are the number one setback for student-athletes. Every year, there are hundreds and even thousands of athletes who have the potential to play at the next level, but they do not qualify academically.

I can not stress this enough. Without the academics, the strategies I'm sharing with you will be worthless. So please do not be the type of athlete who believes success on the field or court will be good enough and that academics don't matter. That can not be further from the truth; just ask around or ask me!

Without going into depth on my story, I'll pick up around January of my senior year in high school. My recruiting was picking up after I sent my highlight video and introduction letter to college coaches personally, which is another story for another time.

My high school coach did not believe I was a D1 athlete. He believed I was too small and needed to find a small school to attend. Luckily, I didn't believe him and took matters into my own hands. To this day, I believe that's the experience that led me to what I do today.

Throughout this book, I'll talk more about my personal recruiting journey in high school, but for now, I want to focus on academics. Going into the spring, it all came down to my one D1 offer from Northern Arizona University.

I remember it like it was yesterday. Coach Axman knocked on the door of my parents' house; we were all excited about the visit. Prior to the home visit, we only had the opportunity to talk on the phone, so after quick introductions, we headed to the kitchen table to discuss the D1 offer.

It was already late in the recruiting process, but NAU had one scholarship left, and it was mine. Coach Axman pulled out a manila envelope with my transcripts in it, and to this day, I have never seen so many red lines and arrows.

He discussed the classes that I had failed early in my high school career and the ones in which I had low grades, and it was the first time I heard about the 16 core classes to be eligible for a scholarship. This is why I prioritize academics with all of my athletes. That was a very traumatic time for the 17-year-old me.

We mapped out an academic game plan so I could get caught up and ideally qualify through the NCAA. I was taking Spanish I and Spanish II, we were making up math classes, and, to say the least, it was very stressful, not to mention the SAT, which I took three times with the hope of a higher score to offset a low GPA.

This was an academic nightmare that lasted through the last day of high school. The experience makes me feel good that athletes are no longer required to take the SAT or ACT to qualify. But in 1996, it was mandatory, and I failed to meet the minimum score to correlate with my 2.2 GPA.

That was when I got the call that NAU had waited as long as they possibly could and would have to give the scholarship to another athlete. Devastating is an understatement. Once again, this is why I stress academics so much and won't even waste my time on athletes who are not taking academics seriously.

Now on to your sophomore year, where things start to get interesting. It is now time to build your athletic brand. At this time, your mindset needs to shift from just being an athlete to being a brand and, better yet, a business.

Some athletes don't grasp this concept because it is relatively new. Athletes have always been judged by their actions and decisions; they have always been held to a higher standard, but now more than ever, maintaining a strong brand is valuable.

Just like any other brand, you must create marketing material that will help you gain exposure. Think about your favorite brands, like Nike, Adidas, and others like Lamborghini. To continue dominating the market, these brands must continue to market themselves in different ways. Athletes should view their brand in the exact same way.

Nike and Adidas use cool commercials with our favorite athletes. Car brands talk about the driving experience and make you envision yourself in that car. I'm sure you're thinking, *What does that have to do with getting a scholarship?* Great question! Now, let's get to the answer.

Just like these worldwide recognized brands, you have to start building your brand as an athlete. In a later chapter, we will discuss NIL, which is all about your athletic ability and the power of your brand.

But for now, I want to discuss branding as a student-athlete who is trying to get the attention of college coaches. Let's start by laying some groundwork and building the foundation for success.

At the start of your sophomore year, you should have profiles on at least two to three social media platforms. This is not to say that you have to wait until your sophomore year, but that is typically when college coaches will start the evaluation process, which will include checking out your social media pages.

My disclaimer is that things change quickly in the social media landscape, so you want to stay up-to-date. But, as of today, I would recommend Twitter/X, Instagram, and YouTube.

I do not have the answer or reason why, but I have personally communicated with hundreds of college coaches on X. For whatever reason, it just seems to be where they hang out the most, so it only makes sense that every athlete with the goal of getting a full-ride scholarship is active on that platform.

My second favorite platform for building your brand is Instagram. This is your day-to-day platform that gives college coaches insight into what type of person you are, what type of things you are into, who your friends are, and what you do with your spare time.

Third on my list is your own TV station on YouTube. This platform takes some work to develop and maintain, but it can be very valuable in the recruiting process and even more valuable in building a recognizable brand. Athletes have successfully used YouTube for DITL (day in the life) videos of a student-athlete. It's also a great platform to share your highlight, training, and other videos that show your commitment to being an elite-level athlete.

## YOUR HIGHLIGHT VIDEO—THE MOST IMPORTANT PART OF YOUR BRAND

Don't let the followers, engagement, or any other factors make you feel like you are on your way to a D1 scholarship. Those are all add-ons to building your brand; if your film does not show D1 offer qualities, I can assure you that your social media following won't matter much at all.

Athletes always ask the same question when it comes to their highlight videos: How soon should I start? There are two perspectives that we can look at to make that decision. With the advancement of social media, iPhones, and access to technology, I am seeing athletes creating highlight reels as young as 10 years old.

If we are talking recruiting and potential offers, my professional opinion would be that college coaches are not evaluating many youth or Pop Warner highlight videos. There are just too many factors that can come into play over an athlete's coming years.

We all know athletes who don't even play the same sport in high school that they played in their younger years. So, if you are creating videos this early with the intention of working toward a scholarship, I can say that you are early. That's not a bad thing; I would always prefer to be early rather than late.

Now, let's flip the coin and go back to one of my original goals for every athlete that I work with. We need to build a brand and build it as big and fast as possible.

That's where that youth highlight video comes in. That's where "parent-managed" social media pages can be beneficial. As a young athlete develops and continues to progress, it's awesome to document along the way. So, if you want to start early, great. If not, great. You can rest assured that starting at 10 years old or earlier will help build your brand, but it does not guarantee a full-ride scholarship will be the outcome.

Next, let's discuss when your highlight video will become the most important part of your recruiting campaign. Here is the best way that I can explain it clearly. If you are an upperclassman on varsity, an under-classman on varsity, or you are competing on a competitive club or travel team, you should be creating highlight videos geared toward recruiting.

Depending on the sport, in most cases, 12U is a very good age to start if you are on a competitive team. Notice the key factor is not age, but the competitive level and the team you are playing on. Not just how good you are, or how many touchdowns, home runs, or points you score. In order for college coaches to evaluate, they are more interested in the competition level than your statistics.

For example, a soccer player can be on their high school team, scoring four goals a game, which is great. However, the competition may not be that good.

The same athlete can score one goal a game on their nationally com-petitive club team, and the coaches will be a lot more excited about recruiting them.

So start the process, edit your film, and begin to build your brand. I'm sure you have many more questions about creating the perfect high-light video, which is why I will be diving deeper into the technical side of your video soon.

In the meantime, just know that your brand is important, but your highlight video is the holy grail of your recruiting campaign.

Academically, as a sophomore, you must keep your grades high and continue taking challenging classes. Sophomore year is also a great time to take the Pre-SAT to prepare for the SAT and possibly the ACT.

Yes, Division I schools no longer require SAT or ACT for athletic scholarships; however, some academic institutions still require these forms of testing. So prepare for them, even if it may or may not be required when the time comes. The goal is for you to be prepared for any scenario that may be presented to you during the process.

Athletically, in your sophomore year, you should be attending more advanced skills camps and showcases. Be sure to include events that will generate exposure and rankings.

During this time, there will be hundreds of options, invites, etc., so be very diligent in researching and determining if the event will be worth attending. Most of these events will highlight college coaches in attendance or have access to the results and film following the event.

These are the key factors that should be used to help you decide what events to attend. In my experience, many college coaches start the athlete search based on these types of events. A few of the more popular groups that host these types of events include 247 Sports, ESPNU, Rivals, and Under the Radar.

Each sport will have its go-to events that have been established and have successfully assisted athletes for years. That's not to say that a newer event will not be beneficial; it's just to say that you have to do your research.

It has been proven that attending these camps can help generate exposure to kickstart the recruiting process, but you have to be strategic when determining which ones to attend. It's also not a secret that many of these events are created simply to make money. They can be a great fundraiser for any program or business, which is another reason to be very selective.

Now, let's talk recruiting. Sophomore year is the latest that I recommend launching your recruiting campaign. This is when you want to create your first list of colleges and athletic programs that align with your skills, academic level, personal goals, and overall potential.

Once you have a solid athlete profile and, most importantly, a very strong highlight video, it's time to launch your campaign and communicate directly to college coaches.

Keep in mind that college coaches may not be able to respond until your junior year, but that doesn't mean you should wait to send them your info. Most college programs are two to three classes ahead in the recruiting process, meaning they have already started to identify the next two to three graduating classes of athletes.

Don't panic, they understand that it is early and the list will continuously change. If you are already a junior or senior, it is not too late. You just have to understand that the recruiting climate is very competitive, so your sophomore year is the time you want to start working your way onto college recruiting boards.

## FOCUSING ON YOUR JUNIOR YEAR

Let's move on to your junior year, and just like your freshman and sophomore years, academics should still be your focal point. This is the year that you want to take the SAT and or ACT, typically in the fall or spring.

In case you didn't know, many students take these tests multiple times to increase their scores. Ideally, you are also enrolled in AP or honors classes to demonstrate your commitment to academics. It's very important that you stay organized with assignment deadlines and testing dates. Junior year is typically the most challenging academically, so you have to be more focused than ever to ensure academic success.

Athletically, it's time to continually update your highlight video and send it out to a minimum of 150 colleges. The two main communication sources will be email and X/Twitter DM. By this point, you should have a pretty clear idea of the college level you can compete on. This is not easy to determine, considering almost every student-athlete wants to play at the Division I level.

Here's what I would recommend as you start to make decisions on which colleges to communicate with. Get with your current coaches, trainers, and mentors and have them evaluate your film and athletic ability.

Ask that they be very transparent about what level they believe you can compete at. This can be very difficult to accept, so only have this conversation with people you trust and respect, and who have a good understanding of the sport and the recruiting process.

There are also people like me who will provide a complete evaluation for a fee, which can be beneficial since it will be unbiased. But that's not necessary if you have the right coaches and people around you. My recommendation would be to use the following grading system for your evaluation: D1-High Major, D1-Mid Major, D1-Low Major, D2, D3, and NAIA.

Once your evaluation is complete, make sure that your highlight video is available online for any college coaches who may be searching. On a side note: make sure to post on your social media channels as well, making sure that everything on each platform represents the kind of athlete a college coach would want to recruit.

When communicating with colleges, keep it very simple. Reach out via email with a brief introduction, your athlete profile, and a link to your video. This is not the time to write an essay to college coaches.

As discussed earlier, college coaches are very busy. Once they like the highlight video and determine that you are a potential prospect, they will then want to learn more about you on a personal level. It sounds kind of cutthroat, but welcome to the recruiting game!

In your junior year, you should still be attending camps and showcases; however, try to focus on events that college coaches will be attending or requesting results from.

Your junior year is also a great time to attend multiple College Camps. These are events that are hosted by the actual college program and run by the actual college coaches.

Here's why this is so important for any athlete trying to secure a scholarship offer. This is one of the few opportunities that a college coach can actually take the time to get to know you, and take you through testing and drills they choose to make an evaluation.

Each coach on the staff will have the opportunity to interact with you, which is great for the coaches' meeting when determining which athletes to offer scholarships to. This is also a good way for a student-athlete to show interest in the program. College coaches know that you have hundreds of choices, so when you attend their camp, it says a lot about your interest in their program.

Before you get excited, let's discuss one of the most important factors when selecting which college camps to attend. At this time, you are going to start receiving a number of invites to these camps. College programs will spend money purchasing lists and databases of student-athletes and start sending out mass invites.

Remember that these college camps are huge fundraisers for the program. There's nothing wrong with that necessarily, but our mission is to get a scholarship, not donate to the program.

Now it's time to focus on your evaluation and what level you can compete at. Let's go back to your evaluation from your coach or mentor that determined which of the six levels of competition you can compete at.

For the sake of this example, let's say that you are a D1-Mid Major potential athlete. As the invites come in, you should focus solely on the D1-Mid Major programs. The goal is to perform and compete in front of college coaches at programs that your evaluation has determined that you can compete at.

Your list of colleges should be updated and ready to go. So if there are D1-Mid Major programs that you may not have heard from yet, now is the time to reach out. Ask for their camp information and show that you are interested in the program. Once you know the level you can compete at, it makes the communication that much easier.

As a parent, I know you're asking how many of these camps your athlete should attend. There is no set answer, but here is how I would narrow down the options.

First, you have to be realistic about the financial burden of camp fees, travel, etc. Outside of that, I would start by ranking each camp in the order of interest in that program.

Next, I would determine the "personal" interest from the actual college program. For example, which schools have reached out to initiate the recruiting process? Which schools have replied to emails, voicemails, and DMs? Basically, try to determine the college programs that really have an interest in you and not just an interest in collecting money.

These are just a few tips to help narrow down the selections. Depending on the sport, many of these camps are in the same general time frame. So start to schedule these as soon as possible to maximize the window of time.

As you start to identify, add, and subtract college programs that fit your athletic and academic ability, continue to reach out. Coaches are bombarded with emails and calls, but that is the name of the game. You have to communicate excessively to get their attention and work yourself onto their recruiting board.

Once you start to create relationships with college coaches, they will take more initiative to make sure there is an open line of communication. This is also a good time to consider unofficial visits to meet coaches and tour college campuses.

To be clear, there are two types of college visits. One is an official visit, which simply means that the college institution will be covering the expenses for the trip for the student-athlete and two parents or guardians.

An unofficial visit means that the financial responsibility is on the student-athlete and family. Here's the secret: make sure to schedule your unofficial visits just like you will do for your official visits.

Let's briefly discuss the difference. Unofficial visits are a great way to let a college coach know that you are very interested in their school. The commitment to paying for your visit can speak volumes to a college coach. Yes, official visits typically mean that the college is highly interested in you attending their school and would love to roll out the red carpet for you. However, like I said, both can be beneficial throughout the recruiting process.

Early in your junior year, make sure that you register with the NCAA Eligibility Center if you have not already. This is important because it will let college coaches know that you are on track to qualify academically and are also eligible athletically to compete at the college level. This is basically an academic progress report for the NCAA.

If you take care of the previous three years of work, you should be walking into your senior year with exposure and, ideally, multiple scholarship offers. That is the ultimate goal, and it does become a reality for a number of athletes around the country.

If that is not the case, don't panic, just keep your foot on the gas pedal. If the offers are not there, continue communicating with college coaches. At this point, you should be even more aggressive with DM, calling, and emailing every coach on your list. This is also a good time to determine if your skill level is not on par with the colleges that you have been communicating with.

For example, this may be a good time to start a new list of D1-Low Major and D2-High Major programs if your original evaluation was D1-Mid Major. If the interest doesn't start to increase and response is not there, there are also D3 and NAIA colleges that are competitive and looking for athletes to help them win.

In today's climate, recruiting for high school athletes can be very difficult. Without going too deep into it, the transfer portal alone has shifted the way college coaches recruit, not to mention the impact that NIL has had on recruiting and attracting athletes.

There have also been a few substantial changes to the number of available scholarships and roster spots throughout NCAA athletics. My goal is not to discourage you, but to be transparent and realistic. You may have to lower your expectations and still accomplish your goal of playing at the college level.

If you are in the select few who are sitting on a few committable offers, congratulations, that is a great accomplishment! And believe it or not, that is rare; the majority of student-athletes do not have offers at the start of their senior year. But if you are one of them that does, now is a great time to narrow down your Top 5 and ideally your Top 3 options.

## SENIOR YEAR, FINISH STRONG

This is not a friendly reminder, but an aggressive reminder that your senior year is not the time to relax. It's actually the exact opposite; it's time to finish strong in every area.

The reality is that in less than a year, you will be a college student-athlete, so you want as much academic and athletic momentum as possible. Maintain your academic focus because college coaches and administrators will be reviewing your academic performance through graduation.

Athletically, continue to play well and compete. You may be in a one-on-one battle with another athlete for your scholarship. What do I mean? I'm glad you asked. Let me explain.

For some college coaches, narrowing down the list of recruits can be very difficult. Let's use the example of an athlete who plays linebacker on his high school football team. There's a college coach who really likes this athlete's skill set. The problem is that there is another linebacker that the coach likes just as much. And the college coach only has one scholarship left for that position.

So what would be the deciding factor? There are a few that I can think of, but I can assure you the coach is studying every play of every game for both athletes. They are trying to determine which one is the best fit for their program.

If it's too close, then the coach will go to the tiebreaker. Academics! The winner is the athlete with the best grades. So stay locked in academically; it will pay off.

Every year, there are athletes who get to their senior year, and it's crickets. There is no response at all from college coaches. If that's the case, let me share a few strategies for that last-minute push.

First, continue to update your highlight video and send it out to colleges. Show how much you have improved since that first communication. This time around, be a lot more aggressive and ask specifically if they are interested or not.

Early on in the campaign, you are focused more on building relationships with coaches, but at this point, you need to know if there are any opportunities. As coaches respond, update your list and keep going. The goal is to get through all the "nos" until you get to a "yes." Don't be afraid to select smaller schools to add to the list.

At this stage, you have to be open-minded; you may be a D3/NAIA athlete, which is totally fine. The goal is to compete at the college level and get your college education paid for, right? So let's keep working to make it happen.

As you work through your college coaches list, you want to determine where the opportunities are and be very transparent when asking questions. Ask specifically if they have any scholarship offers remaining. Ask if there is any other financial assistance available. This will not only get you to the answers you need but also show the college coach that you are highly interested in making this work and joining their program.

As you narrow down opportunities, carefully review the terms and requirements. At this stage, there is no such thing as too many questions.

Now it's time to make your final decision and formally commit to a program. Typically, this means signing a National Letter of Intent (NLI) for NCAA schools.

You have successfully made it to the transitional period of this book. Now is the time to take notes as we progress through the details of your recruiting campaign.

# CHAPTER 3

# BUILDING AN ATHLETIC PROFILE

Let's get into the meat and potatoes of getting that scholarship. The starting point is your Athletic Profile, which is essential in showcasing your talents, achievements, and potential to college coaches.

We will start with your basic information. You should include your full name and contact information, including email, phone number, and social media handles. Also, include your high school name, sport, city, and state along with your graduation year. Don't forget to add your travel team, 7v7 team, or any other competitive team that you compete with.

The next section should include your physical attributes, which will vary based on sport—height, weight, position(s), and relevant metrics such as 40-yard time, vertical jump, etc., that are specific to your sport.

Academic information is standard for each sport. You want to include the following:

- Core-course GPA, weighted and unweighted, if available
- Standard test scores, such as SAT and ACT, if applicable, and high school honors courses

- AP classes that display a high academic aptitude, and all other academic honors and achievements throughout your high school career

Now let's look at your athletic achievements and statistics. College coaches love to see your stats. They want to determine if you are a dominant athlete in your area, so include statistics, both seasonal and career stats, and accolades, including awards, all-conference, all-state, MVP, etc. It's also a good rule of thumb to add key tournaments or major games, such as state championships and titles.

Full transparency—the next section will more than likely be the most important thing on your Athlete Profile. It's your highlight film. Every time I think of a highlight video, a quote from one of my favorite movies, Maximus in the 2000 movie *Gladiator*, comes to mind: "Are you not entertained? Is this not why you are here?"

This is a great perspective on the goal of your highlight video. It must be entertaining to a coach. Let me be clear about what I mean by entertaining. I'm not talking about graphics, screen transitions, and fancy titles.

Coaches must be entertained by your skill. In seconds, they must see that you are a good fit for their program. They must be entertained enough to make it to the end of your highlight video.

If we are being honest, you can have all the stats in the world, but that doesn't guarantee that you are a D1 athlete. The flip side of that coin is that you might not have all the stats in the world, and your film can still get the attention of college coaches.

Let's talk about some key components of an "entertaining" highlight video: Keep it short and focused; aim for two to three minutes in length. Coaches have very limited time and thousands of highlight videos to evaluate, so it's very important to make sure every play is a strong highlight. One mistake that I see often is the "build-up" highlight video. It starts slow and gets better as it goes.

Here's a secret. You are not making a movie, and most coaches will never make it to the end. So, start the video with your best plays. Grab their attention early and keep it.

Also, try to highlight different, but relevant skills. For example, if you're a basketball guard, show your shooting ability, defense skills, and passing ability. Try to demonstrate versatility within the sport and position.

It's important to only use high-quality footage. I can't tell you how many videos I have watched that were filmed on mom's iPhone. There's nothing wrong with filming from an iPhone, but if mom is into the game, shaking, losing the ball in the video, please do not use it.

One simple suggestion is to get a tripod from Amazon and let someone film who doesn't really care about the game (like a little brother or sister).

This next one can be difficult, but don't worry, it's not mandatory. But if you can get multiple angles, that would be great. College coaches like to see the play develop, and sometimes multiple angles can help. This will not be the difference between a scholarship or not, but just an add-on that can help coaches see your game.

For clarity and simplicity for college coaches, make sure to highlight yourself on the video. There are a number of software programs that can help with this. It can be as simple as a circle or arrow that indicates where you are on the screen.

The last thing you want is the coach watching your video and not being able to determine where you are. So before each play, use an arrow, a circle, or a spotlight effect to identify yourself. Make sure that they are not too distracting; the simpler the better.

We briefly discussed this earlier, but let me be clear. Please avoid distracting effects and music. I prefer that you don't use transitions at all. Keep it simple; let your plays entertain and not your creative editing skills, unless you're a film major and you want to highlight that … just kidding. No edits.

This is something that most people never think about. Once your film is complete, get feedback before sending it to college coaches. Show your video to coaches or mentors to get their honest feedback. Be sure to communicate the purpose of the video and that you need them to evaluate honestly.

This will serve two purposes for your recruiting mission. Number one: You can make changes before sending it to college coaches to make sure it's the best representation of your athletic skills.

Number two: We discussed earlier how you can determine what level you can personally compete at. For example, you can ask the coaches or mentors who are evaluating your film what level they believe you can compete at before sending it to college coaches. They must be trusted and honest, which also means you have to decide if you want to use their evaluation to determine which schools you will communicate with. You are basically using them to ensure that your list of colleges matches your ability to play at that level.

Considering how important your highlight film is in this process, I wanted to provide more detail and a checklist that you can follow.

## 10 KEYS TO A GREAT HIGHLIGHT FILM

### 1. Keep It Short and Engaging.

- Length: 2-3 minutes max is ideal. Coaches don't have time to watch long videos, and most athletes don't have more than three minutes of "really good" highlights.

- Start strong: Place your best plays in the first 30 seconds to grab their attention immediately. This is not a movie; don't try to build momentum. Wow them from the first play!

- Avoid fluff: Focus only on impactful moments that highlight your skills and potential. Don't include B-roll or extra random footage.

## 2. Showcase Relevant Skills.

- Position-specific skills: Include plays that demonstrate the key skills needed for your position (e.g., agility for a wide receiver, vision for a point guard).

- Diversity of skills: Show a range of abilities like scoring, defense, assists, and include some variety if possible. For example, if you're a running back, show your runs, but include catching the ball as well.

- Game situations: Use footage from real games rather than practice or drills to demonstrate your performance under pressure.

## 3. Ensure High-Quality Footage.

- Clarity: Use HD video with good lighting and no shaky camera movements. Parents! Hire someone if needed. Coaches don't want to watch film that will lead to a headache.

- Visibility: Clearly identify yourself using an arrow, circle, or highlight at the beginning of each play.

- Sound: Remove background noise or commentary if it distracts from the visuals, and do not add music. Coaches evaluate film for a living; they will not be impressed by your music selection.

## 4. Structure the Video.

- An introduction is not needed. Get right to the highlights so the coach can start the evaluation process.

- Name, graduation year, school, and position should be included in the title or text. It should not be on the actual highlight video. Save this for the email, DM, or your attached athlete profile.

- Include physical stats (e.g., height, weight) and GPA if it is strong. Once again, this can be in the email, DM text, or included in your athlete profile, but not on the actual highlight film.

- Entire content should be 2-3 minutes.

- Arrange plays by starting with the most impressive. Critique every play and remove any that do not represent you as a college athlete.

## 5. Edit Professionally.

- Simple transitions: Use clean cuts; avoid flashy effects or overediting.

## 6. Seek Feedback.

- From coaches: Ask your high school or club coach for input before sharing.

- From teammates: Sometimes, peers can point out strengths or weaknesses that you might have overlooked.

- From scouts and recruiting consultants: Ask for an evaluation of your highlight video.

## 7. Update Regularly.

- Fresh content: Replace outdated footage with new highlights as you improve. This is a very important step that every athlete should do. You can create a new video or update an existing one, depending on how many highlights you have.

## 8. Common Mistakes to Avoid.

- Long clips: Cut plays down to only the action; avoid unnecessary buildup.

- Low-quality footage: Avoid blurry or hard-to-follow clips.
- Irrelevant plays: Exclude moments that don't showcase your strengths.

### 9. Distribute Effectively.

- Platforms: Upload to YouTube or Hudl for easy sharing. Use a descriptive title like "John Doe | 2028 | Basketball | PG/SG | Highlight Reel."
- Share with coaches: Send the link directly to coaches via email or through direct messaging on social media.
- Social media: Post on platforms like Twitter or Instagram, tagging schools and coaches where appropriate. By following these steps, you can create a highlight video that effectively markets your abilities and makes a strong impression on college coaches.

### 10. Progression.

- Your video should showcase your progression throughout your high school career. If you are an underclassman, coaches will evaluate you as such. But they will expect you to get substantially better throughout your career, which means your highlight video will also get better over time.

### Final Thoughts

Don't send your film too early, and don't be afraid to send it. That sentence was created to confuse you, so let me explain. Don't waste college coaches' time and blow your first impression by sending film that is not on par with the division or caliber of the program. Number 6 above is a good guide to determine if your film should be sent or if you should continue to improve and build your highlights.

Once your film is ready, be aggressive and get it out to as many college coaches as possible. I would also recommend following up aggressively to ensure your film is being evaluated.

Once your film is locked, loaded, and ready to go, the next step is to create a shareable link. This can be as simple as uploading your film to YouTube or utilizing other platforms like Hudl. The key is to simply have a link that college coaches can click on to watch your highlight video.

Other than your contact information, it's a good idea to include your high school or club coaches' contact info as well. Once a college coach is interested, they will want to contact your coach to get more detailed information about your play and your character on and off the field.

I've been doing this for 20+ years, so I understand that the relationship with your high school coach may not be all good. I'm not here to judge whose fault this may be, but I wouldn't be doing my job if I didn't say, "Fix it!"

Whatever it is, it has to be fixed. Now, on the other hand, you can add the coach who loves you to your athlete profile, but I can assure you of one thing. You won't get a scholarship offer without the college coach talking directly to your high school head coach or club team head coach.

So I will say this one more time. Fix it. All it takes is one bad conversation, and you will never hear from that college coach again.

For your first optional addition to your athlete profile, you may want to include reference letters, which can have some impact, especially when communicating with Division III and NAIA colleges. On those levels, most athletic programs rely heavily on admissions to get student-athletes accepted into the college, so multiple reference letters can be very beneficial in this scenario.

Talent is important, but visibility is critical. Coaches must know who you are and what you bring to the team.

**What coaches look for:**

- Physical talent (speed, size, strength, agility)
- Technical skill (position-specific abilities)
- Coachability and attitude
- Academic performance
- Highlight video and game film
- Verified stats and accolades

**Action steps:**

- Create a highlight video showcasing your best plays.
- Upload your film to platforms like Hudl or YouTube.
- Use email and social media (Twitter, Instagram) to promote yourself.

# CHAPTER 4

# HOW TO COMMUNICATE WITH COLLEGE COACHES

Now, let's go even deeper into the best practices for reaching out to college coaches.

Reaching out to college coaches effectively is a crucial step in the recruiting process. Here are some best practices to increase your chances of getting noticed and earning a scholarship.

One of the biggest mistakes that I see is student-athletes waiting to start communication with college coaches. In my experience, I have talked to coaches who are two to three years ahead on their recruiting board, which means that they have already identified the student-athletes they want to recruit before the end of their sophomore year.

Keep in mind that there are recruiting rules that may prevent a college coach from reaching out that early. Still, it doesn't mean they can not initiate the recruiting process by communicating with your high school and club coaches, scouts, etc., to gather the information they need.

So I would recommend beginning to reach out during your sophomore year of high school, or as early as your freshman year if you are competing at a high level.

One rule of thumb is the level at which you are competing. For example, if you are a freshman playing on varsity at your high school, that's usually a good sign to start sending information to college coaches early.

If you are on a highly competitive club team and playing above your age group, that's another example of a good time to start communication early. The key is having enough high-quality film to get their attention and get your name added to their recruiting board.

When initiating the recruiting process, it is very important to research the right programs. One of the first questions to ask is whether the program is a good fit for you. Identify the programs that match your athletic ability, academic interests, and personal goals. You should know the team's style of play, recent achievements, and scholarship availability.

Once you identify the programs, gather contact details for the coaching staff, usually available on the school's athletics website. This is where organization will prevail. Start a list of colleges with coach contact info, so that you can track the colleges you are communicating with.

Remember, this process is ongoing, so it's all about adding and updating this list as you work through the process. We have already talked about creating a professional athletic profile, but it is important enough to talk about again.

Make sure you include all pertinent information, such as name, graduation year, GPA, standardized test scores, and contact info. Include your athletic position, stats, awards, accolades, and highlights. You can also include your academic highlights, like honors and AP courses you have completed.

Remember, you have to keep this short and sweet, so don't go too far with information. College coaches have limited time to evaluate each athlete. Ideally, they want a snapshot to determine if you are a recruitable athlete.

To complete your athlete profile, you must add your highlight video link. If your highlight video is not complete or not good, WAIT. Don't waste the opportunity to get a college coach's attention.

We stress academics and all the other attributes to get a full-ride scholarship, but let me be clear. If you cannot play at the next level, or don't have the film to show that you can play at the next level, there's a very high percentage chance that you will not hear from college coaches after sending your athlete profile.

For now, continue laying the groundwork to communicate with college coaches. One of the original forms of communication is still relevant today—sending a personalized email to initiate the recruiting process.

Let's break down the email and discuss exactly what should be included:

- **Subject line:** Use something specific like "John Doe | 2025 Forward | 4.0 GPA | Las Vegas, NV." This should be a simple but effective line that gets a coach to open the email.
- **Introduction:** Briefly introduce yourself, including your name, class year, and position. Once again, do not write a book. This should be a paragraph at most.
- **Why their program:** Mention why you're interested in their school and team. Include at least one sentence that shows you are interested in that specific program. "Congrats on going 8-2 last season." Something simple that also says that this isn't just a copy-and-paste email.

- **Attach athlete profile and link to highlight video:** Make sure the athlete profile is in a PDF format or digital to avoid any issues with opening it. The highlight video link should be from YouTube, Vimeo, or Hudl, basically a platform that ensures there will not be any issues watching the video.

- **Call to action:** Politely ask if they are recruiting for your position and request feedback. This is very important and helps you to update your college list as you work through the recruiting process.

## *Example:*

Subject Line: John Doe | 2025 Forward | 4.0 GPA | Las Vegas, NV

Coach [Last Name],

My name is [your name], and I'm a [year in school] forward from [High School/Club Team]. I've been following your program and admire [specific quality about the team]. I'm interested in contributing to your program's success while pursuing [specific academic interest] at [School Name].

Last season, I [specific athletic stat/achievement]. I've attached my athletic profile and highlight video for your review: [insert link].

I would love to hear your thoughts and learn more about your recruiting needs for [your graduation year]. Please let me know if there's a good time to connect.

Thank you for your time,

[Your Name]

[Contact Information]

Once you start this process, it is imperative that you manage and maintain all your social media channels. The first step is to go through each one and delete any and everything that will not help you get a scholarship.

If it's questionable, delete it. If you have to think about it, delete it. Your social media must maintain a clean and professional presence. College coaches are known to creep on social media.

This means that once a coach has some interest in you, their main priority is to determine what type of person you are. Not just what type of athlete, but what kind of character you have.

Use platforms like Twitter and Instagram to post updates, showcase your training, nutrition, pre-game, post-game, and connect with coaches. Show your community outreach, and talk about studying, as well as the challenges of being a student-athlete. Show them the type of athlete and person they are getting if they get you.

Let me prepare you now. This is called the recruiting process because it's just that—a process. If you don't receive a response within one to two weeks, send a polite follow-up email. Like I've mentioned before, college coaches are very busy, so a nonresponse is not a no. Set your calendar reminder and follow up.

In sales, one of the first things that is taught is the follow-up. Even though you may not feel like it, you are selling yourself to these college coaches. So stay persistent, professional, and respectful without being overly aggressive. We are talking about consistent, not overbearing, communication, so don't miss this point.

Attending college camps and showcases is another opportunity to communicate with college coaches to build a relationship. My advice is to make sure you are prepared mentally and physically. This may be your only opportunity to build a relationship and perform in front of that coaching staff, so take advantage of it. At the end of the day, be prepared with some questions, and be ready to showcase your skills and work ethic.

As mentioned earlier, make sure to track communication throughout this process. Use a spreadsheet to keep track of which coaches you've contacted, their responses, and next steps.

This is usually unspoken, so I'm going to discuss it anyway. Be honest and truthful about your stats, achievements, and interest level. Coaches value integrity. By following these steps, you can make a strong impression on college coaches and increase your chances of earning a scholarship.

# CHAPTER 5

# LEVERAGING THE POWER OF NIL (NAME, IMAGE, LIKENESS)

**O**riginally, this was going to be a bonus chapter, but I decided to share some NIL insight early because the new landscape of NIL is now a key factor in the recruiting process.

Before we get into it, let me start with a quick introduction to name, image, and likeness. The term NIL refers to the rights of student-athletes to earn money or receive other forms of compensation by using their personal brand, which includes their name, image, or likeness.

NIL deals allow athletes to benefit from their status and marketability without jeopardizing their amateur status in college sports. Here is a basic introduction to what NIL means and how it works for student-athletes.

**Name:** The right to use an athlete's name in promotional or commercial activities (e.g., having their name appear in a social media ad).

**Image:** The right to use an athlete's picture in a media ad, campaign, or other marketing material (e.g., on a poster, product, or in advertisements).

**Likeness:** The right to use an athlete's persona or identity (e.g., video game avatars, shout-outs, or endorsements).

NIL essentially lets athletes monetize their personal brand through endorsements, sponsorships, appearances, and other opportunities.

Then there is revenue sharing. Revenue sharing for college athletes is a system where a portion of the money generated by their athletic programs—such as ticket sales, TV deals, sponsorships, and merchandise—is distributed directly to the athletes. This allows athletes to receive financial compensation for the value they help create, while still competing at the college level.

Why is this important?

First of all, this is a great financial opportunity for athletes. NIL rights open the door for athletes to earn money while still in school, helping them build financial security and learn business skills. This also incentivizes athletes to constantly work on building their brand.

I love the fact that if an athlete is focused on building a brand, they typically understand that they must stay out of trouble and always show good character.

This is also important for the recruiting process. With the emergence of social media, college coaches are doing their homework behind the scenes. Coaches are looking at what you post, what you share, and your comments. They understand that social media will give them a good idea of the character of the athlete they are recruiting.

In summary, NIL represents a groundbreaking shift in college sports that allows student-athletes to profit from their personal brand. By understanding and navigating NIL effectively, athletes can maximize their opportunities and set themselves up for success on and off the field.

Now that you have dollar signs in your eyes, let's discuss some NIL rules and regulations to watch out for. While the NCAA permits NIL deals, each state and school may have specific rules that athletes must follow. This means that athletes must ensure their NIL deals comply with both their school's and state's rules to maintain eligibility.

The last two factors of NIL that I want to share are time management and the one that no one wants to talk about, taxes. Student-athletes already have a very difficult time balancing their schedules, so be very conscious of the workload NIL deals can bring.

Lastly are taxes, and in my opinion, this is the most important or dangerous area of NIL. Once you secure your first paid NIL deal, I would advise you to schedule a meeting with a tax advisor, CPA, or lawyer.

This is preliminary, but I would prefer that you are ahead of this before owing tons of money in taxes and not being prepared. The right consultant will discuss setting up business entities, bank accounts, tax deductions, etc., to make sure you are compliant. The last thing you want is the IRS knocking on your college dorm room door.

# CHAPTER 6

# THE ROLE OF PARENTS

Parents, you play a crucial role in supporting your child through the recurring process. But the key is to help without overstepping. As a parent, it is natural for us to want to do everything for our children, knowing that's not the recipe for long-term success.

So let's discuss how you can support and provide resources without becoming a crutch or crippling your student-athlete's development. The recruiting process is typically a student-athlete's first experience preparing and developing a campaign to "sell" themselves to college coaches.

Generating interest from a college coach is similar to searching for a job and going on an interview. So, consider this an intro to the real world.

Now, let's discuss the role of parents in this process. The number one area that parents should focus on is learning about the recruiting rules, eligibility requirements, and timelines for divisions (NCAA, NAIA, NJCAA).

For example, did you know that there are only certain times during the year when college coaches can contact athletes? There are also times when college coaches can evaluate, and these annual calendars are based on the division of the college programs.

Be sure to visit ncaa.org and save the Recruiting Calendar for your student-athletes' sport. Also, make sure that it is the most current calendar available.

It will also be valuable for parents to have a clear understanding of the specifics of athletic scholarships, including what full and partial scholarships cover. These can be very confusing for a family that has never been through the recruiting process, so the more clarity that you have, the better.

Hopefully it's not too late, but I would also be very wary of recruiting services that make big promises and simply add your student-athlete to their large database, hoping for the best.

Please don't be fooled into thinking that a fancy website is the secret to getting a scholarship. It's not; it's the continual work that you, the parent, and the student-athlete are willing to do to be successful.

The only guidance you should require is a recruiting strategy that is specific to your student-athlete. That should not cost you $5,000-$10,000 per year! Do your research, ask around, and make the best decision for your child. Recently, I had a conversation with a parent of a student-athlete who has been with a recruiting service for nearly 18 months. When we scheduled the Zoom call, I thought they were new to the recruiting process and wanted some guidance.

In reality, they needed help after investing thousands of dollars with a recruiting service. Not to mention, they were on a contract that could only be cancelled if their child had a severe injury that ended his athletic career. This may not represent all of the recruiting services, but it is very common.

There are also "Street Agents" to look out for. People who brag and boast about how many college contacts they have and how they will guarantee scholarship offers if you're willing to pay. This is illegal based on the current NCAA rules and can put the student-athlete in danger of being ineligible.

One of the red flags that is common amongst street agents is paying for offers. The NCAA prohibits any recruiting services from being compensated for a specific result or outcome. If you hear that you'll be paying a certain amount of money for each offer, run away as fast as you can.

If you do find that you need or prefer to have assistance through this process, you can schedule a free consultation with me or one of my team members. At that time, we can start to create your student-athlete's recruiting strategy.

The first thing that we make clear is that there are no guarantees in this business. Legitimate recruiting companies like ours will discuss your potential, but we will never guarantee that an athlete will get a scholarship simply by paying us.

Another common red flag is simply stating, "Pay this much and we will do all the work." As great as that sounds, are you willing to put 100% of the responsibility in their hands? That's not an ideal game plan in my opinion, especially knowing that college coaches would 100% prefer to hear from the student-athlete over a "paid" recruiting service. Enough said on that topic, let's move on.

Another area parents should be heavily involved in is camps, showcases, and other recruiting events. The easiest way to determine if a camp or showcase is valuable for your student-athlete is if it provides meaningful exposure, skill development, and recruiting opportunities. Depending on your athlete's grade, it could be one of these, or ideally, it would be all three.

Depending on the sport, the most valuable camps and showcases are the ones that college coaches attend, actively recruiting in person. Camps hosted by the actual college can also be beneficial. We recently traveled with a group of athletes from Las Vegas to Oregon. The event was for high school football players in grades 9-11. There were 75-100 college coaches on the field evaluating athletes. This created so much value and resulted in dozens of athletes receiving scholarship offers, including ours.

However, as I mentioned earlier, these camps are also great fundraisers for college programs. But that doesn't mean that you should not attend; it means that it should be a college program that has an interest in your student-athlete or a school that your student-athlete has an interest in.

The only addition to that would be a school that your student-athlete has the ability to compete at. Be realistic when making decisions about what camps to attend. Lastly, before committing, make sure to verify that the actual coaches will be there to evaluate. In many cases, these camps are evaluated by third-party companies, which doesn't mean it's a complete waste of time; you just want to be evaluated by college coaches directly when possible.

In some sports, such as football, college coaches are not permitted to attend camps in person during certain times of the year. In these cases, we must rely on third-party evaluations, which means you need to research the company to make sure they are credible.

A couple more characteristics of camps and showcases worth attending include quality skill training. Typically, the camp will promote the coaches who will be running the skills portion of the event. This is a great way to do your research and determine if they indeed can teach your student-athlete and provide personalized feedback.

The feedback should also include areas of improvement. In fact, I would prefer that to be the only feedback. This provides an instant opportunity to get better.

Another way to determine if the camp or showcase is a good fit is the overall competition level. Attending a camp or showcase with high-level competitors lets your student-athlete be measured against top players to see where they stand.

Competing with higher-caliber athletes can also help you get noticed by college coaches. There is no better way to evaluate an athlete than by watching them compete against other high-level athletes. I'll be remiss if I don't mention that as a parent, you should make sure the level of play aligns with your student-athlete's skill level. Some showcases are for top-tier talent, while others cater to athletes of all levels.

## CONCLUSION

I want to leave you with a few more ways to maximize the camp or showcase experience. Make sure the event allows filming, and it's even better if they provide professional videography services. That way, your student-athlete's best reps can be added to their highlight video and social media channels.

Many showcases also include seminars on recruiting, training, or academic preparation, helping athletes understand the full spectrum of college sports. As you can see, the goal is simple: make sure that it is worth the time and money before making a decision.

When it comes to communicating with college coaches, most parents want to take control of this process. However, that is a mistake. I know that you know your athlete better than I do, but this is a great time to see their commitment to getting a scholarship.

Here's what I know to be true. College coaches are ok with hearing from people like me. People who have taken the time to evaluate an athlete to determine what level of competition they can compete at. The goal is to make a college coach's job easier by only providing information on athletes who have been evaluated and can compete at their particular college.

After the initial communication, most college coaches want to hear directly from the student-athlete to gauge their interest in the college program.

With that said, the person they don't want to hear from is mom or dad. You are your student-athlete's biggest fan and number one supporter, which makes it very difficult not to be biased. So, parents, my advice would be to let your child initiate and control the communication with college coaches. Your job is to oversee and make sure they are following up and staying consistent. Fight the urge and temptation to take over the process, even if it hurts a little.

Now, let me get you back in the game with two areas that you and your student-athlete should work on together. The first is researching colleges.

As a family, you should be exploring schools that align with your child's athletic level, academic interests, and personal preferences. Discuss realistic options based on skill level, program fit, and the type of school environment they'd thrive in.

Let me warn you ahead of time. Don't be surprised if your student-athlete wants to go to college across the country. Don't think they are trying to escape and never see you again. Ask the right questions to determine if this is a real and realistic goal or if it just sounds good. Make sure to communicate what that would look like. Mention key factors, such as being homesick, which is very common, and the cost of flights to come home for holidays or for family to travel to games.

Once these topics are discussed, the family can then decide which schools to pursue.

The second and final is providing emotional support throughout the process. I know that sounds simple and is a no-brainer, but let's remember this is the most important transition of your child's life. It's also a long process that in many cases isn't complete until the end of an athlete's senior year.

During the process, they will have to focus on academics, playing, training, and recruiting, as well as maintain some form of personal life.

They will also have the comparison complex, seeing other athletes getting offers and committing to universities while your child is still sending emails. So don't underestimate the emotional impact this process will have.

Parents play a crucial role in the scholarship journey. Support, guidance, and realistic expectations are key.

**Parent action items:**

- Stay informed about NCAA rules and deadlines.
- Help your child create a time management plan that balances academics and athletics.
- Be proactive in helping your child research schools.
- Attend college visits and ask the right questions.

# CHAPTER 7

# COMMON RECRUITING PITFALLS AND HOW TO AVOID THEM

Navigating the recruiting process is exciting, but it can be filled with potential pitfalls. Here are a few more red flags that athletes and their families should look out for to ensure they're making the best possible decisions.

Something that has become increasingly popular is coaches offering scholarships without being clear or transparent about the details of the offer. It is very important for you to ask the right questions when you receive verbal offers from college coaches.

One of the most important questions is a new one. Over the last few recruiting seasons, I've seen athletes getting offers sooner than ever. For someone like me, this is great; there's no better feeling than when one of our athletes gets their first scholarship offer.

I'm sure you're wondering why that is a red flag when that is the ultimate goal. For college coaches, recruiting is all about strategy. They have recruiting boards with dozens of athletes, all ranked by position. To be clear, that is the goal; as an athlete, you want your name on that board.

Now for the part that can get a little bit misleading. Many coaches will contact nearly all of the athletes on their official recruiting board and offer scholarships. The problem with that is some of those offers are non-committable. What does that mean exactly? It means that the school is highly interested in you becoming a part of their program. But they are still in the recruiting process and therefore can not allow you to commit at this time.

As I said earlier, recruiting for college coaches is all about strategy. So what better way to show an athlete they are highly interested in them than to make an offer?

That's how they look at it, and to be honest, I think it's a pretty good strategy, and here's why. If I'm a coach and I'm interested in an athlete, but I'm not 100% sure if they are a good fit, why not make a non-committable offer and continue to recruit the player and get to know them? The key is transparency, which, from my experience, some coaches give to the athlete and family, but others don't.

If a coach offers a "scholarship" but doesn't specify whether it is committable or not, then you need to ask. If the offer is committable, the next question is whether it's a full or partial offer. Some coaches may talk about scholarships in general terms without committing to a specific financial offer. Be very cautious if a coach pressures you to commit without providing details about the scholarship, amount, duration, or renewal terms. Remember, this is a business transaction, and the terms of the agreement matter.

Once the details of the offer are provided, athletes and families usually have one question in mind. Should we commit? This is a personal question, so I can not answer it with a simple yes or no.

One thing we have to remember is that this would only be a verbal commitment. The scholarship offer is not truly accepted until the NLI

(National Letter of Intent) is signed. A verbal commitment can be retracted at any time.

Before committing, I *can* offer pros and cons, other options, and a type of analysis that every family must consider. Location, climate, academics, and competition level are just a few key factors to think about.

I also want to talk about the pressure from coaches to commit early. Coaches who push you to decide on the spot or say that offers will disappear if you don't commit quickly may be using high-pressure tactics. My advice would be to analyze the timeframe, your other offers, and what athletes may have committed to that school recently. These will help you determine if this is a tactic or a reality.

In some cases, college coaches may have multiple offers out, and the first to commit is the one who will get the scholarship. I don't want you to panic and make an impulsive decision, but I also don't want you to lose an offer after all your hard work. So to be clear, a legitimate offer should give you time to consider, discuss with family, and weigh options carefully.

Some colleges are considered "academic" schools, which typically means they have a much higher focus on academics. But every university should make it very clear that academics are important and that you will have all the support you need to be successful.

If the program seems focused solely on athletics without clear academic support and resources, that could indicate a lack of commitment to your overall academic and career development. If they do not mention it, ask questions about tutoring, study hours, and support systems to ensure academics are prioritized.

Let's talk about communication, one of my favorite topics. In the defense of college coaches, I will continue to say that they are very busy. College coaches typically work 12-16 hours a day, six days a week, and there really is no such thing as an offseason.

Now that we have that out of the way, inconsistent communication is not acceptable. Coaches who are difficult to reach, who miss scheduled calls, or who frequently change plans may not be reliable.

Don't get me wrong, life be life-ing, so we all get it. But you are making a decision to spend the next four to five years at this school, which means consistent, clear communication from coaches is important, and a lack of it can be a red flag regarding their professionalism or investment in you as a recruit. This is a very exciting time, but don't be blinded by the light and miss these red flags.

Another key factor when deciding on which program to commit to is player turnover and overall poor team culture. Here's my disclaimer for this topic. When evaluating, you must account for the transfer portal and its impact on athletes who transfer for many different reasons.

When evaluating, you need to dig deep to understand the reasoning behind athletes transferring from one school to another. Is it based on playing time, maybe a new recruit who came in, or are they just unhappy with the program overall?

As you dive into the reasoning, you can make the best decisions possible. Understand that high transfer rates, lots of players leaving the program, or poor team morale can be warning signs of a toxic culture. One of the best ways to get the inside scoop is to talk to current and former players. That way, you can get an honest assessment of the team environment, the coach's style, and the support available.

This is why official and unofficial visits are so valuable. If a coach doesn't encourage you to take official or unofficial visits or makes it difficult for you to explore campus facilities and meet staff, it might be another sign they're hiding something.

Visiting a campus and meeting with staff, professors, and current players is crucial for understanding the environment and facilities. These are very important factors when deciding where you will spend the next four to five years of your life.

We all like to believe we are the best athlete on the planet, but 99% of the time, that is not true. As athletes, we have one goal: to continue to get better. Be wary of exaggerated promises about playing time, starting positions, or fast-tracking to the pros. Not that these are not possible, it's more about a coach making these promises while you are still deciding what school to commit to. As mentioned before, the recruiting landscape is very competitive. Some college coaches will make promises that they will never deliver on.

We all want to start when we get to a college program, and that should be your mentality and goal. But understand that college coaches say a lot of things, and that doesn't guarantee they will come to fruition. So the best approach is to look for honest and realistic expectations and try to exceed them. Most coaches will take this approach. They will describe in detail what they have planned for your future, the position they want you to play, the playing time, and how you fit their system. These are all great and will help you narrow down your options. However, if the promises start to seem unrealistic, keep your guard up.

Another red flag tactic is when a coach encourages you to end communication with other programs before you're ready to make a final decision. It's essential to keep options open until you're certain about your commitment. Avoid burning bridges with other schools. You never know what is going to happen and when you may need that relationship. College coaches talk to each other and have no problem sharing their experience with certain athletes.

For example, earlier I mentioned the transfer portal and how it has changed the way college coaches recruit. That's another reason why relationships are so important. Most coaches get hired and fired multiple times throughout their careers. You never know which school the coach will land at, so keeping a strong relationship can come in handy in the future.

We discussed academics earlier, but let's take a different approach and view academics from a different perspective. When it comes to making a decision, there are a few things that you should look out for academically. Low graduation rates or a poor academic reputation can indicate that a school prioritizes athletics over academics, which could jeopardize your long-term success. Check the graduation rate of athletes in your sport and ask about the academic support provided to ensure you're choosing a program that values education.

I know what you are thinking. You're going to be a pro athlete, so you don't need your education. That's a great goal to have; it's a goal that will keep you focused through college. But the reality is that less than 2% of college athletes actually go pro.

Here's the point of my message: Even if you make it to the pros, you will spend more of your years not being a pro athlete. Why not be prepared and educated for the next chapter of your life? Even during your professional athlete career, it's important to be educated financially and in other areas to help make the best decisions for your future.

So many athletes trust accountants and lawyers to handle all of their finances, only to discover that they have been taken advantage of. Or they simply do not have the financial literacy to manage the millions of dollars earned throughout their career. Did you know that approximately 78% of NFL players face financial stress or hardship within just two years after leaving the league? And about 60% of former NBA players are broke within five years of retirement (per a 2009 *Sports Illustrated* article).

Last, the red flag I want you to consider is coaching stability. If a program is undergoing a coaching transition or has a history of frequent staff changes, it may lack stability, which can impact your athletic and academic experience.

There is an upside to a new coaching staff. That can be a great new start for a program, and the new coach may really be the one who will take the program to the next level.

In college sports, turnover is inevitable. In most cases, when a head coach is fired, that means his entire staff is gone as well. In some cases, a staff member may be hired by the new head coach, but that is rare. Here's some perspective to help navigate.

You have to determine if you are willing to be a part of that hopeful future or if you are looking for more stability. If it's a new coach, ask about their previous experience, record, etc. Do some research to see what type of coach they are and determine if it's a good fit.

# CHAPTER 8

# HANDLING SETBACKS, INJURIES, AND DIFFICULT TRANSITIONS

Now that we have established some of the recruiting pitfalls, it only makes sense to address the inevitable. Handling setbacks, injuries, and difficult transitions is a significant part of an athlete's journey. It's not about avoiding them because we will all run into them at some point. Let's discuss how to attack them head-on and navigate the difficult times.

The first thing to recognize is that it's normal to feel frustrated, discouraged, or anxious at different points in your career and life. Please accept that it is normal to have an emotional response to a major setback, especially one that takes you away from the sport you love.

When these times come, the worst thing you can do is deny the emotional response. Avoiding denial and acknowledging the reality of a setback helps you create a realistic plan for growth and recovery. I'm also a big fan of seeking professional help when needed; I share that from firsthand experience.

In terms of injuries, consult qualified sports medicine professionals for diagnosis, treatment, and rehabilitation plans. The faster you take this step, the faster you can return to play. With today's technology, there are not many injuries that an athlete can not return 100% healthy from.

As athletes, we tend to fight through everything or refuse to show weakness. However, that is the recipe for a short athletic career. You should immediately seek a professional for any and all injuries that may potentially or have already removed you from competition. This may sound obvious to some, but trust me, it's not as common as you think.

Follow your rehabilitation plan meticulously, including physiotherapy, rest, and a gradual return to training and eventually to competition. While going through the recovery process, engage in alternative workouts that maintain fitness without risking reinjury, for example, swimming, yoga, or pilates for low-impact training.

Along with that, there is the importance of nutrition. A proper diet and hydration will aid in faster healing and overall wellness.

As athletes, we are leaders. We tend to work through the difficult times and make it look easy. We tend not to communicate our internal issues to avoid looking "weak."

That can be the furthest thing from the truth. When it comes to mental health, there is no such thing as going through it alone. If at any point you feel a mental decline or severe negative emotion, that is not a time to figure it out on your own.

Just as you would when you have an injury and seek a sports medicine doctor, physical therapist, or trainer, you need to speak to a sports psychologist or counselor to address the emotional impact of setbacks, family issues, relationship issues, or any other things that have a negative impact. Don't take this for granted; it may be the most important section of this book.

Here are a few mental strategies that every athlete should include in their "get back on track" plan. Have a positive mindset by focusing on what you can do instead of what you've temporarily lost.

One example is to use downtime to improve mental skills. This is a great time to practice visualization, study more film, and take mental reps. I also recommend setting goals. Take the professional's recovery plan or mental health plan, and set goals that you can focus on accomplishing. Achieving small goals can boost motivation and confidence. Depending on the severity, this can be a long process. It's imperative that you focus on small goals that will lead to a big comeback.

As you get older, this next one will make more sense. But the sooner you can practice it, the better. Gratitude. Practice gratitude by reflecting on the things you're thankful for to maintain perspective and reduce stress. No matter how severe, there is always something to be grateful for; you just have to find it.

Now, let's finish this out with a few more strategies to overcome any setback that you may come across. During these trying times, it's important to stay involved with your team, even in a limited capacity, to maintain a sense of belonging and purpose.

Keep your support network very close. That includes family, friends, and mentors for encouragement and accountability. Reflect on the people who have helped you along your journey and stay connected to them—the people that you know will stay positive and motivate you through your recovery.

Another important piece to this puzzle is community engagement. Participating in events, workshops, and community outreach can not only keep you positive but also give you that sense of gratitude I discussed earlier.

We tend to get in our heads when we are going through troubled times, but remember, there's always someone going through something worse. Trust me, I know that's not what you want to hear in the middle of turmoil. But it is reality and can be powerful in helping you work through the issue.

If you can utilize these strategies, setbacks can become learning opportunities. You can evaluate what led to the setback and identify ways to prevent similar issues in the future. You can work on your areas of weakness or neglected skills during downtime, such as studying game film or enhancing communication skills.

Don't forget to celebrate the small wins. Recognize and reward progress, no matter how small. This will be key to your ability to stay motivated throughout the process. Whether it's hitting a rehab milestone or adapting to a new mental strategy, every step forward should be celebrated. Setbacks should be viewed as temporary and part of the growth process in both sports and life.

Once you fight through, don't forget the experience. Share your journey through speaking opportunities and social media. This not only motivates others but also helps you process and find purpose in your challenges.

Handling setbacks effectively is about balancing resilience, resourcefulness, and support. With the right mindset and approach, you can emerge stronger and better equipped for future challenges.

# CHAPTER 9

# SUCCESS STORIES AND INSIGHTS FROM FORMER SCHOLARSHIP ATHLETES

As I think about my 20+ years of helping athletes accomplish their goal of playing at the next level, there are a few stories that always come to mind.

Brandon Marshall was a sophomore at Cimarron High School in Las Vegas when we met. At first sight, there was nothing that would've said NFL, but Brandon's work ethic was five-star for sure. He had the goal of playing at the college level and was willing to do whatever it took to accomplish that goal.

We created a game plan that included strength training, speed training, supplements, and a recruiting strategy. The most impressive part was the fact that he committed 100% to the plan. As you can imagine, that is not the case with all of my athletes.

After his junior season, we submitted Brandon's name for the Nike Camp in Southern California. The camp was invite-only and very difficult to get into.

After being denied, Brandon and I did not give up. We continued to push the issue, and eventually, we got the green light to attend the camp. Just another example of what determination can get you if you're willing to keep going. For me, it was easy to keep pushing to get the opportunity, since Brandon had been so committed and consistent up to that point.

Brandon went on to be named MVP for the Linebacker group, and that was the kickoff to what became multiple offers and eventually a commitment to the University of Nevada Reno. Did I mention that he then went on to play 11 seasons in the NFL and win a Super Bowl with the Denver Broncos!

Another athlete of mine who dominated the recruiting world was soccer player Hailey Gordon. Hailey was special from the first day she walked into the building. She had all the tools that suggested this was not only a D1 athlete, but a pro if she continued to develop.

She quickly became one of the hardest-working athletes that we have had the chance to work with. She was also one of the youngest athletes in the program, so we knew we had plenty of time to develop and accomplish some major goals.

Being that Hailey was a standout, we focused the majority of our recruiting game plan on branding. Her parents did the research that we discuss in this book and found the best showcases for her to attend to maximize her exposure. They even had her guest play on elite travel teams in Southern California, even though she lived in Las Vegas. Not to say that everyone should do this or needs to do this. It's just an example of doing what it takes to accomplish the overall goal.

Hailey is also a dual citizen of the US and Mexico, which allowed her to play on the Mexican National Team at the age of 17. I told you she was special. Hailey is now a freshman at the University of Georgia on a full-ride scholarship and maximizing her NIL opportunities. Once we recognized that she was elite, it became all about exposure to college coaches and building her brand.

This book is titled *D1 Offers*, so I wanted to share a couple of D1 stories. We agreed in chapter 1 that the goal was to play at the collegiate level, so I'm just as proud of my D2, D3, and NAIA athletes who accomplished the mission and went on to compete and have a great college experience after working through the recruiting game plan.

# CHAPTER 10

---

# RECRUITING RECAP—
# TIMELINES AND STRATEGY

The goal of this chapter is to simplify the steps and strategies to generate exposure and get scholarship offers. To simplify the strategy, we will look at each year of high school and focus on three categories.

1. Academic
2. Athletics
3. Recruiting

Here's a year-by-year simplified strategy to help you secure a full-ride scholarship. If you are a sophomore, junior, or senior, take the time to go through each year and compare your progression to the timelines and strategies in this chapter. If you realize you are behind, don't give up. Get more aggressive and get caught up.

## FRESHMAN YEAR

**Goals:** Establish a strong academic foundation, start building athletic skills, and learn about the recruiting process. Most families only go through the recruiting process once or twice, if they are lucky. So it's important to learn as much as possible. I wrote this book to close the gap and hopefully take some of the confusion out of the recruiting process.

## 1. Academics

- Aim for strong grades from the start; colleges will look at all high school years.
- Take challenging courses, particularly in core subjects (math, science, English, and social studies). Align your courses with the 16 core course requirements.
- Begin developing study habits and time management skills, balancing academics and athletics. This is a skill that you will utilize for the rest of your life.

## 2. Athletics

- Focus on skill development and training specific to your sport. It's time to lock in on the sport and position that you want to play at the next level.
- Join the high school team and consider club or travel teams for additional exposure. In most sports, college coaches evaluate club or travel footage more than high school footage. So, depending on the sport, your travel/club season can be more important than your high school season for recruiting. I'm currently working with an athlete who did not compete in AAU basketball until her junior year, went on to have a great senior year, and now I'm trying to convince coaches that she can play at the next level. They love her high school film, but the competition level is not very high, so they can't understand why she did not play AAU, as that is where the best competition is.
- Begin attending camps or clinics, if possible, to develop skills and gain feedback from coaches. This can include showcases,

recruiting camps, or team camps. Just do the research to assure it's worth the time and money.

## 3. Recruiting

- Learn about the recruiting process and eligibility requirements for NCAA, NAIA, and NJCAA. This is very important considering you only have four years to complete your academic requirements.

- Set goals for both academics and athletics, considering the level of play you want to pursue. As a freshman, I believe you can accomplish any goal with four years of preparation. So, decide what division you want to compete in at the college level and get to work.

## SOPHOMORE YEAR

**Goals:** Maintain academic progress, build an athletic resume, and start gathering footage. This is when things get serious in terms of communicating with college coaches.

Most college programs are identifying potential recruits as early as ninth grade, and some even earlier. So don't wait to start communication with college coaches. They also understand that you are still developing. The goal is to show them that you have the potential to compete at the collegiate level.

## 1. Academics

- Keep grades high and continue taking challenging classes. Meet with your school counselors to ensure that you are on track academically in terms of course requirements.

- Take the Pre-SAT as a practice for the SAT, which can become valuable for admissions into the more "academic" focused programs. It's true that some programs no longer require the SAT or ACT as a prerequisite for admission, but there are still a number of programs that do. So I recommend taking the SAT and/or ACT; regardless, it can even result in more scholarship money for your college education.

- Identify any areas where you may need academic support, and get help if necessary. No matter what you do, do not wait to ask for help. Time is not on your side when it comes to academics in high school. So, as soon as you recognize that you are struggling in a particular class, immediately ask for academic support. That can be a tutor, time after class with the instructor, or a classmate who has proven to be successful in that class.

## 2. Athletics

- Begin recording games and practices to build a highlight reel. Include a mix of skills and in-game performance. This can also include performance and skill training videos. That's a great way to show college coaches that you are committed to getting better on a daily basis.

- Attend more advanced camps and showcases to compete at a higher level. Now it's time to level up and compete with the best of the best. This will serve two purposes: showing college coaches you can compete with the best and giving you areas of improvement.

- Develop relationships with high school and club coaches who can support you in the recruiting process. Contrary to popular belief, it is not your high school coach's job to help you get a scholarship. If they do, that is a bonus, and you should be very appreciative. Most club coaches do focus more on recruiting, which only enhances their club program, so make sure to communicate with both about your aspirations to play at the college level.

### 3. Recruiting

- Research colleges and athletic programs that align with your skills, academic level, and personal goals. The research should be based on the overall college experience, not just athletics and the number of games won. You need to start thinking about location, weather, career goals, social experience, etc., not just the sport.

- Create an athletic profile with a minimum of your class, position, stats, athletic and academic awards, GPA, and contact info, along with any other pertinent information. This does not have to be a two- to three-page resume; it can be something simple, typically one page, that provides a college coach with an outline of the type of student-athlete you are.

## JUNIOR YEAR

**Goals:** Now it's time to increase academic rigor. You should already be actively reaching out to college coaches and preparing for standardized tests like the SAT and ACT.

### 1. Academics

- Take the SAT and/or ACT in the fall or spring; many students take these tests multiple times. This is a great opportunity to unlock academic scholarships and grants.

- Enroll in AP or honors classes, if possible, to demonstrate academic dominance. Once again, this can unlock more academic money, which is always a good thing.

- Stay organized with assignment deadlines and test dates, as junior year is often the most challenging academically. There's no turning back at this point, so maximize every minute to ensure academic success.

## 2. Athletics

- Continue to update your highlight video and make it available online to college coaches. You should already be communicating with college coaches through email and social media outlets like Twitter (X). Communication should include your athlete profile along with a link to your most recent highlight video. To create the link, you can upload your video to YouTube, Vimeo, or create your highlight video on Hudl if that is an option.

- Continue participating in showcases and camps, especially those attended by college coaches and scouts. This is the time you want to be very strategic in determining which camps to attend. Consider the relationship with the college coach, the recruiting response, or if it's an opportunity to prove to a coach you can compete at their university.

- Start compiling a list of references from coaches or trainers who can speak to your abilities and work ethic. Some college coaches will contact each reference when they add you to their recruiting board. Others will simply make cold phone calls and emails to learn more about who you are as a person. We talked about it earlier, but let this be a reminder that your character is more important than your athletic ability.

## 3. Recruiting

- Continue to reach out to college coaches via email and social with brief updates, your athletic profile, and new video highlights. College coaches are very busy, so keep it simple. Don't send them an autobiography about your life. Keep it short and simple. Once they start recruiting you, they will ask more personal questions to establish a stronger relationship.

- Attend unofficial campus visits to get a feel for different schools and their programs. This is something that athletes don't take advantage of enough. Yes, official visits are better because the school is paying for the trip expenses. However, unofficial visits show college coaches that you are highly interested in their program. This also gives you the opportunity to experience more time on campus, which will ultimately help you make the best decision.

- Register with the NCAA Eligibility Center if you're targeting NCAA Division I or II programs. Once you are registered, you will receive an NCAA ID Number. This number helps college coaches determine if you are on track academically and eligible to receive an athletic scholarship. So once again, this is another example of you taking care of business in the classroom.

## SENIOR YEAR

**Goals:** Continue the recruiting process until you are satisfied with the offers or options that you may have. If you do not have offers at this time, it would be smart to initiate the process of submitting college applications. This can be a good time to select a few colleges that you are interested in and inform them that you have applied to their school and would love to be a part of their athletic program. Once admission is approved, it can lead to a partial scholarship offer or a possible walk-on opportunity. As discussed earlier, the goal is to have your college education paid for, and this can be one way to achieve it.

### 1. Academics

- Maintain grades, especially in your final semesters, as coaches will review your academic performance right up until graduation. Don't make the mistake of letting off the gas now. Finish strong!
- Complete college applications by the deadlines, including essays and letters of recommendation, but also continue the recruiting process.

- Ensure all transcripts and SAT/ACT scores are sent to colleges and the NCAA Eligibility Center, if applicable.

## 2. Athletics

- Continue to train and perform well, which will help avoid injuries; this is a crucial season for final evaluations, so you want to perform at your best.

- Update your highlight video with new footage and key moments from your senior season. Show college coaches your final stage of development and make it clear that you are continuing to get better.

- Attend official visits if invited, and be prepared to ask questions about scholarship offers, program expectations, and support for athletes. If you do not have any official visits, start to schedule unofficial visits to learn more about college programs.

## 3. Recruiting

- Follow up with coaches to express continued interest or to finalize any remaining steps. Make sure they take the time to watch your final highlight video. Stay aggressive during this time; it may come down to you and one other player, so the most aggressive and consistent athlete will win.

- Be clear on scholarship offers, and carefully review the terms and requirements. You don't want any surprises; you will be packing your bags in a few months, so make sure all details are clear and confirmed.

- Make your final decision and formally commit to a program, typically through a National Letter of Intent (NLI) for NCAA schools. This is the time to celebrate! All the hard work has paid off, and you and your family should be very proud.

This roadmap provides a structured path to staying on top of both academic and athletic demands, helping you position yourself for scholarship success. Remember, this is a process and will not happen overnight. It's important that you take every minute of high school seriously if your goal is to get that full-ride scholarship.

There are two types of athletic scholarships: head count and equivalency.

**Head Count Sports** (full scholarships):

- Football (FBS), basketball (men's and women's), tennis (women's), gymnastics (women's), volleyball (women's)

**Equivalency Sports** (partial scholarships):

- All others (e.g., baseball, soccer, track)

*Additional Tips:*

- Apply for FAFSA and other financial aid.
- Look into academic and need-based scholarships to stack with athletic aid.

# CHAPTER 11

---

# PREPARING FOR CAMPUS VISITS

In my opinion, this is one of the most important parts of the recruiting process. Preparing for official and unofficial visits to college campuses is a critical step for student-athletes. In my experience, this should be one of the main factors in making a decision on which school to attend. Visits will give you, the student-athlete, and your parents a realistic idea of what attending that school would be like.

Here's the information that you need to make the most of these opportunities. Remember, you must take advantage of every minute on each college campus.

Before we get started, let's define the different types of visits as they pertain to recruiting. Let's start with official visits (OV), which is the goal and what athletes get super excited about.

This is a visit to a college campus that is paid for by the school. These visits are more formal and are often only utilized for serious recruits. It's an opportunity for a college program to roll out the red carpet and display how badly they want you to commit to their program.

When a college schedules an official visit, it will cover travel, lodging, meals, and entertainment expenses. The visit will typically last up to

48 hours for most college divisions. One key factor when it comes to OVs is that you are limited to five official visits to NCAA Division I schools, but you can only use one visit per school.

You can see why student-athletes have to be so selective when it comes to official visits. Many college coaches will ask where their program is on your college choice list. They are simply trying to determine how serious you are about their program in particular. Official visits are limited and expensive, so ideally, you should focus on your top college choices.

For Division II and Division III schools, there is no limit on official visits; however, they usually have a more limited budget for OVs. In recent years, there have been talks of removing the limitations on official visits for Division I programs as well. I would not be surprised if we see that change very soon, allowing unlimited OVs for all divisions. In my experience, it only makes sense, and here's why.

Most highly recruited athletes have 10-plus offers, and even after narrowing their list, there are usually more than five schools that they have a high interest in. As I mentioned earlier, OVs are a great time for college programs to roll out the red carpet. They will invite you to the big game, make sure that alumni are in attendance, and set up your locker with a game jersey and all.

They want you to get the feeling that this is the place for you. The entire staff will know your name, you'll meet other recruits, and you'll be on the field or court for pregame. I mean, it's going to be an experience if it's done right by the college program.

Now that you have gotten all excited about taking your first official visit, let me bring you back to reality. You are only allowed to take OVs after the start of your junior year of high school for D1 and D2 schools. Coaches change, programs change, so it only makes sense not to take an official visit too early. As discussed before, turnover is very high in college sports. So the coaches that may be recruiting you early in your high school years may not even be at that school by the time you graduate. Be patient and continue to learn more about the process and keep working.

But don't worry, there are a lot of things that you will need to do before you start scheduling official visits. One of them may be to schedule unofficial visits (UV). Even though I know the recruiting process is confusing enough, let me recap exactly how unofficial visits to colleges work.

The biggest difference is that an unofficial visit to a college campus is paid for entirely by you, the recruit, and your family. That includes your travel, lodging, meals, and entertainment expenses. The only thing that a college can provide is complimentary admission to home games. This may not sound as exciting as an official visit, and I'm not going to sugarcoat it. An OV is better than a UV, but UVs play a large role in the recruiting process and should not be taken for granted. An athlete should not base their decision simply on an official visit experience. OVs are all about the wow factor. The schedule is full, the excitement is high, and everything is set up to impress you. Unofficials will be fun as well, but in my experience, they are more realistic, which helps you make the right decision when selecting the college to attend.

Unofficial visits do not have a time restriction of 48 hours like official visits. So as a recruit, you can take more time to get to know the staff, players, and campus. There is also no limit on how many unofficial visits you can take. Once you start to narrow down the college choices, you can take as many visits as needed.

One of the key factors to keep in mind is that you should always schedule UVs with the college staff. You want to make sure they know you are coming for a visit, and make sure they have the time to notify compliance with NCAA contact periods before scheduling travel, etc. Unofficial visits typically will include campus tours, meetings with coaches if it's prearranged, and attending games or practice. In my experience, I love both OVs and UVs for all of the athletes that we work with at Phase 1. Here's why both are important and should be utilized.

Official visits provide a deeper, all-expense-paid look into the school's athletic and academic environment, usually for athletes who are seriously being recruited. During OVs, there is a lot of smoke and mirrors, and bells and whistles that college coaches hope you are inspired by. I've seen names on jumbotrons, custom jerseys, photo shoots, promo videos, and that's just the beginning.

When a college decides to schedule an official visit, not only are they serious about recruiting you, but they also know that other schools are just as serious. So be prepared for an experience of a lifetime when you take these official visits.

Unofficial visits allow you to explore multiple schools on your own timeline. They allow you to get to know the staff and campus at your own pace and visit as many times as you would like. Even though UVs have to be scheduled, in most cases, you will get a more realistic view of the athletic program and the school.

Of course, college coaches will still try to impress you into a commitment; it just won't have all the allure of an official visit due to NCAA limitations. Both types of visits are valuable tools, and I recommend taking advantage of both if possible.

Your goal is to assess a potential fit academically and athletically. Use your visits to make an informed decision, and don't be in awe of the red carpet rollout. Remember that when you commit and show up for day one, there will not be any red carpet, bright lights, or screaming fans, just your coaches and teammates ready to work. Now, let's get more detailed on the things you need to focus on before your official or unofficial visits.

It always amazes me how many athletes don't do this. You are trying to determine where to spend the next four to five years of your life, yet many don't take the time to research the school and program. In reality, this should be the first thing that you do early in the recruiting process.

I'll start with the location, facilities, and population. You're an athlete, I get that, but don't be so enamored by the team's success that you don't think about the location.

Every year, I get a couple of calls from athletes who are homesick and want to transfer or, even worse, come home. Some of these calls are a result of the transition of moving away from home, but some are legit.

It's a different world when you are thousands of miles away, can't just go home when you want to, and your family has to plan their visits weeks in advance. Some athletes may want or even need to be as far away from home as possible, and in some situations, I recommend it. So I guess what I'm saying is that you need to know which one you are.

In terms of academics, you should have a clear understanding of the majors, classes, and resources available for your field of interest. Some of you may be thinking, *I don't have an academic interest yet.* That's fine and understandable, so you should still research the major and degree programs that the school is known for.

Almost every college in the country has an academic program that they are known for or specialize in. Your research could lead to helping you discover what you would like to study once you arrive.

We can all agree that the goal is an athletic scholarship, but I would also research the graduation rate for student-athletes at that school. This can be a clear example of the resources and support the school provides its athletes with. Yes, there are many factors that contribute to athletes graduating, but this will serve as a good baseline to compare schools.

This should be the easy part of your research. Learn as much as you can about the overall athletic program, but you want to emphasize your sport. Learn about the team's recent performance, previous season, recruits they are interested in, and what seniors are graduating.

This research will become very valuable throughout the recruiting process. Knowing which athletes will be on the roster when you arrive and what big-name recruits they may be bringing in can be very valuable. I'm not implying that you should run from competition; I'm suggesting that you should know your competition.

Just to be clear, you are in competition. Once you walk on campus, you're just another athlete fighting for a starting spot. It's going to make you think back to those official visits and red carpet rollouts, only to realize that it's only sweat and tears from this point on. So don't arrive with an entitled mentality, that will be a big mistake that will be very difficult to overcome. From day one, show the coaching staff and team that you are here to contribute to the success of the program, not just your own selfish agenda!

As you deep dive into the roster and recruits, don't forget about the coaching staff. Starting with the head coach, you want to know their coaching style. I'm not talking about X's and O's, I'm talking about how they communicate, the culture, the feeling when your head coach walks by you.

This is so important for athletes to research. Not all coaches are best for all athletes. Some coaches are disciplinarians, while others yell a lot and may even curse you out on the sideline. Some are so laid back that you couldn't tell if they were winning or losing. This style may be hard to get a read on, which can be difficult for an athlete.

One of the best ways to process this is by thinking about your high school or club coach that you resonate with the most. Which coach has been able to get the most out of you as an athlete? That should give you a glimpse into the type of "coach personality" that may get the best out of you in college.

Now, let's get even deeper into the research and look at the playing style of each team. Playing style includes the X's and O's, including the type of offense and defense the coaches run. In a simplified answer, what offense and or defense fits your abilities?

The good thing is that most college coaches make this assessment prior to initiating the recruiting process with an athlete. One of the first questions they ask is if this athlete fits their system. Once they know the answer is yes, the recruiting game begins.

This does not mean that you should not make the same evaluation. Ideally, you need to be in a system that fits your current and future athletic ability. I know this is sounding like a lot of work, but I'm here to tell you that it is all necessary work. This is a very serious decision that you are making at a very early age.

The transfer portal makes it seem easy to leave if you are not in the right program or at the right school, but let me tell you, it's not that simple. The athletes who have the best response after entering the portal are the ones who played consistently and contributed to the program they are now trying to leave.

Here is a simple way to look at the transfer portal. College coaches typically begin the recruiting process when an athlete enters the transfer portal. They want to see films, statistics, attitude, and more before offering the opportunity to transfer. So if you are not a contributor, understand that the portal will likely not be a good option for you, unless you plan on going to a lower division, which is totally acceptable.

This may sound like a no-brainer, but you will be surprised. Throughout your visit, coaches will always ask if you have any questions. So let me be clear, the answer should never be "No, I don't." Since you are making one of the most important decisions of your life, you should probably have a few questions ready to go. To help you with this process, I will give you three categories to create questions from:

1. Academics—Ask about the graduation rate of the athletes at that school.
2. Athletics—What type of system does the head coach run, and does it fit your playing style?
3. Lifestyle—What do the athletes here do during their free time?

Yes, it is that simple. The goal is to have questions ready to go that relate to the current topic of the visit. For example, you can ask about the class schedule, whether most of your classes will be early in the morning, or if they will be spread out throughout the day. Is tutoring or study hall mandatory, or is it based on your GPA? Do athletes have a specific academic advisor that they will be working with directly? These are all simple, but great, questions that will help you make the best decision and impress the coaches.

Athletically, inquire about the training and practice schedule.

> *Is it rise and shine at 6 a.m. for workouts, or will the training be after class? Are we able to study film at any time, or do we only study film as a team?*
>
> *What's the team culture?*
>
> *Do most of the athletes get along?*
>
> *As my coach, what expectations do you have for me?*

Lifestyle questions are just as simple but effective. Ask about housing options.

*Do I have to stay on campus my freshman year? What other campus activities are there during the school year?*

*Does the local community support the team and school athletics?*

Now that this chapter is twice as long as I thought it would be, let me give you five takeaways to ensure you maximize your official or unofficial visits.

### 1. Be professional.

- Dress appropriately: Wear business casual for meetings and comfortable clothes for campus tours. Show college coaches what type of athlete they are recruiting.
- Polite communication: Address coaches, staff, and players respectfully. Don't walk in with a casual demeanor; it can be terrible for first impressions.

### 2. Observe closely.

- Team dynamics: Pay attention to how players interact with coaches and each other. These will be your teammates if you commit to that program.
- Facilities: Evaluate training facilities, locker rooms, and academic support centers.
- Campus atmosphere: Imagine yourself living and studying there daily. Try to get a feel for the day-to-day experience and determine if you would be comfortable or not.

### 3. Participate fully.

- Attend events: Participate in team meals, campus tours, or class visits if offered. Especially on official visits, don't disappoint the staff by not attending an event they have had planned for weeks.

- Engage: Ask questions, show genuine interest, and take notes. I also advise my athletes to take pictures, as it will help them remember each experience.

## 4. Get to know current athletes.

- Questions to ask: Ask about their experience with the program, coaching style, and campus life. Try to get an honest opinion and ask multiple athletes to get a better perspective.

- Culture fit: Gauge if the team environment aligns with your values and goals. Can you see yourself hanging out with athletes on the team?

## 5. Take notes.

Seriously. My athletes look at me crazily when I say to take notes. But here's why that is important. After your fifth official visit and your ninth unofficial visit, everything will start to run together. You'll be mixing up schools, coaches, and experiences. People will ask how your visit was, and all you'll have to say is that it was cool.

Taking notes will give you the advantage and ability to relive each experience. My advice would be that you take notes every night before going to sleep. That way, everything is fresh on your mind.

After the visit, it's important to show your appreciation. You should send thank-you notes to multiple coaches with whom you are establishing a relationship. This can be by email, DM on social media, or a phone call.

One rule of thumb is to utilize the same form of communication that you have been using prior to your visit, unless you now have personal phone numbers. So if you have been texting, text the thank you. Also, be sure to be specific by referencing a specific highlight from the visit.

If you now have personal cell phone numbers, for example, send a thanks for the number and thanks for the specific highlight of the visit.

Once the thank you message is sent, it's time to reflect on the experience. List out the pros and cons of the visit. Ask if any of the cons are deal breakers. This will gradually eliminate some schools and highlight others.

Now it's time to stay in touch with each coach and continue the recruiting journey. Continue to send out updates, new film, etc., to show you are still highly interested in the program.

By preparing thoughtfully, engaging fully during the visit, and reflecting carefully afterward, student-athletes can make informed decisions about where to continue their athletic and academic careers. Please take this very seriously and do not make an impulse decision.

# CHAPTER 12

---

# WHY PATIENCE IS IMPORTANT

Patience is a crucial virtue during the recruiting process for several reasons. The first is very simple: the process takes time. Each coach's recruiting timeline will vary, even when they may be recruiting the same athletes as other programs. Different colleges and coaches operate on unique schedules, and offers may not come immediately.

I've worked with some college coaches who only offer scholarships at in-person team camps and events. Others only make offers on official or unofficial visits. It's their way of determining if you are interested in their school or if you are just stacking up offers.

You must always remember that college coaches have to protect their interests as well. They have to feel confident that the offer and continued relationship building are worth it. Think about how many athletes receive offers and have no intention of committing to that program. So, patience is key as you wait for the offers to roll in.

In comparison, by level of play and division, Division I programs may make offers earlier and expect an athlete to commit earlier as well. The top programs are basically competing against each other for recruits, so they are typically a little more aggressive, since the potential recruits are more limited.

On the other hand, Division II, III, or NAIA schools often decide later in the process, which allows them to see what athletes may have slipped through the recruiting cracks. If you look at the process unbiasedly, it makes sense that smaller schools will be more patient as they watch athletes receive offers and ultimately commit. They are hoping to find athletes who have the potential to play at a higher level; however, the offers did not come in.

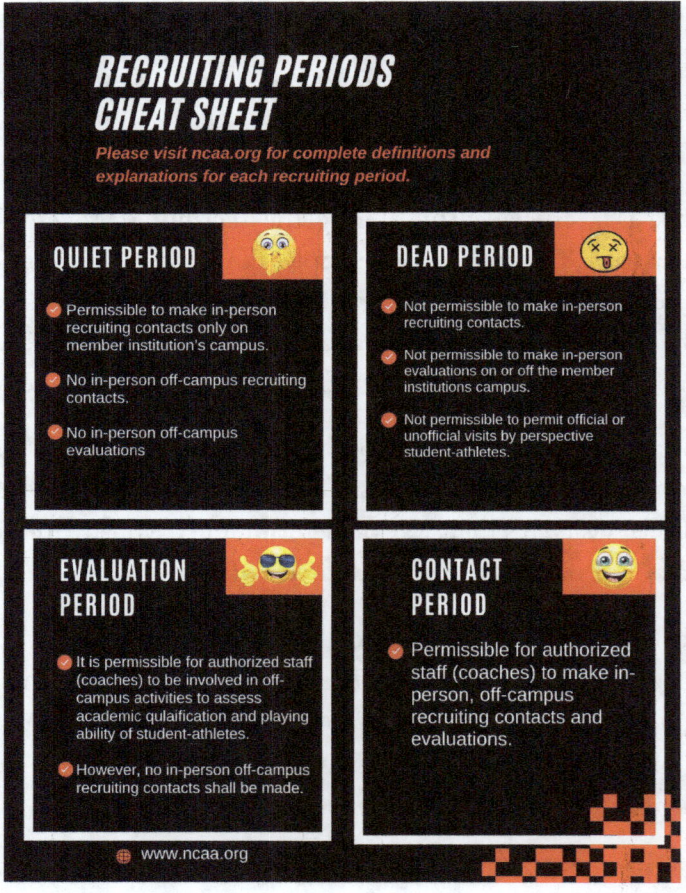

As you work through the recruiting process, you also have to factor in the different periods for your sport. There is the quiet period, dead period, evaluation period, and contact period.

To help you and your family understand each of these periods, I've included the definition of each as defined by the NCAA. The goal is for you to understand the different periods, so that you have different expectations throughout the year.

Coaches also need time to evaluate multiple athletes through game film, camps, live performances, and academic qualifications before making decisions. So, there are times of the year when coaches may seem very quiet. That can simply mean they are evaluating, or they may be in a period where they can not contact you at all.

For example, it may be a dead period, so they are just quietly evaluating film. A dead period means that it would be an NCAA violation to contact you, even if they wanted to.

Recently, one of my athletes was pouring out their soul, feeling down and out because they were not hearing from college coaches. I pulled up the recruiting calendar available at ncaa.org, and sure enough, it was a dead period. The athlete was relieved and continued to work through the recruiting process.

Patience is also very important when it comes to building relationships between coaches and athletes. Your number one priority should be establishing trust and rapport. If selected carefully, these are lifetime relationships that you are creating. This is an essential part of the recruiting process, and it doesn't happen overnight.

Coaches want to see consistency in performance and character over time, and you should be looking for the same. How is that coach performing? How is their relationship with their players? Yes, you have to be proactive and work toward building these relationships, but it will be more than worth it.

I wouldn't be the transparent person that I am if I did not mention that competition is intense. There are no restrictions on where a college coach can recruit.

If you ever want to do some extra math, here it is. How many high school [your sport] teams are there in your city and your state? Now, how many teams are there in the country? How many players on those teams play the same position as you? That number is how many athletes you are competing against, so it's very safe to say that scholarships are limited.

Only a small percentage of high school athletes will ever earn a scholarship, especially full rides, and the competition for those spots is intense. Coaches must weigh all their options carefully, and some really take their time.

One of the silent factors that many athletes don't think about is waiting for openings. Sometimes, athletes need to wait for other recruits to commit elsewhere before a spot becomes available. This sounds rough, but it's just how the game goes.

College coaches will say, "He or she is on my list" or "On my recruiting board." Trust me, that's a good thing; you want to be on that recruiting board. But if you have not received a committable offer, it could mean that you are number 4 or 5 on that list. It's still not a bad place to be, but it may require more patience and an occasional woosah to work through it.

Let's discuss what I believe to be a part of the development process of an elite athlete. First of all, you are learning in real time how to make informed decisions. To successfully navigate the recruiting process, you must explore all options. Rushing into a commitment might mean overlooking better academic, athletic, or cultural fits at other schools.

Patience allows athletes to visit campuses, meet teams, and assess whether a program aligns with their overall goals. It teaches resilience and stick-to-it-tiveness (I made this one up). The process of handling delays, rejections, setbacks, and not hearing back from a coach or being passed over for a roster spot will definitely mold and shape you for the future.

While waiting through this process, my advice for all my athletes is this: Continue to focus on developing your skills, academics, and personal growth. This will be a great story to tell when you are my age.

As you have already realized, I like to be as transparent as possible. This process will be very stressful for every athlete, not just the ones who do not receive an offer early, but also for those athletes who have multiple offers. Of course, you would rather be the one with multiple offers, but my point is that this process is very stressful for everyone. If you find yourself without an offer, keep in mind that some athletes receive offers late in the process due to coaching changes, roster adjustments, or standout performances in senior seasons.

The moral of the story is to keep working until it's all said and done. And even then, there are walk-on options, junior college options, and small schools where you can ball out and enter the transfer portal. So if this is really what you want, be willing to do whatever it takes to accomplish your goal. It really is that simple.

# CHAPTER 13

# PREPARING FOR LIFE BEYOND COLLEGE SPORTS

We all have the hope and dream of going to the league. I've personally been in the middle of over 50 athletes making it all the way to the professional level. However, I've worked with over 1,000 athletes, so you don't have to be a math major to see how small that percentage is.

My advice would be to start preparing for life beyond sports as early as possible. Not to mention that even if you make it to the pros, you'll more than likely spend more years of your life not competing than you spend competing. So why not be prepared either way? Although you may not see it now, being that you have more than likely not even graduated from high school yet, trust me, time flies when you're having fun. So, preparing is a critical step for student-athletes to ensure long-term success.

Let's get into some practical strategies to help you transition effectively. From the start, your focus should be on and remain on academics. Of course, I want you to become the best athlete possible and have a great career, but not at the expense of your academic success.

When it's time, select a field of study that aligns with potential career interests beyond sports. Make sure to prioritize not only grades but also relationships with professors, which can be crucial for future opportunities.

The college athlete's schedule can be rigorous, but I still advise that you explore internships to gain real-world experience in your areas of interest. In most cases, this can be done during the off-season or summer breaks.

Engaging with alumni is another way to help secure future career success. Take the time to interact with former athletes and non-athlete alumni through school networking events or websites like LinkedIn. You should also make it a point to attend career fairs that are designed to connect student-athletes with employers.

When it is time to transition, utilize your school's career center for guidance. Typically, they will be able to assist with resume building, interview preparation, and even job placement. They also host events on campus that can be very beneficial to your future career goals.

Throughout the year, a number of workshops are offered on career planning, financial literacy, and overall professional development. These can catapult you into your career if you take them seriously and take advantage of them.

As we close out this chapter, let me give you three additional areas of focus that I know will have a significant impact on your future.

The first is to learn budgeting skills. Learn to manage money effectively to prepare for life without athletic scholarships, stipends, or NIL deals.

Second, start to build an emergency fund that will cushion the transition into "the real world." This can be as simple as a savings account that you save money in throughout your college career.

Last, find a career mentor in your desired industry for guidance and advice. These three alone, along with the intangible skills that you develop as a collegiate athlete, will ensure you are prepared for the transition. Your time management, leadership, and communication should continue to improve, which will translate into any career in the future.

As you embark on life beyond sports, be open to new opportunities. You may want to consider pursuing a master's degree or professional certification. Just make sure it is in a field that you are interested in. Current studies suggest that 40-50% of college graduates are not working in the area of their major. So the earlier you can determine "what" you want to do, the better, but understand that the answer may change.

You may have heard the phrase, "Once an athlete, always an athlete." I, for one, believe this is true. With that being said, you should also look into alternative careers in the sports industry. You can explore roles in coaching, sports administration, broadcasting, or athlete performance training. There's also the realm of sports management, sports marketing, and, of course, the Jerry Maguire role of a sports agent. All of these will keep you connected to sports, and your experience as an athlete will automatically give you an advantage.

We have spent a solid amount of time talking about careers and potential opportunities. There's also the other side of the coin, which is entrepreneurship. Just as in a traditional career, you can use the discipline and perseverance developed in sports to build your own business.

I will be the first to tell you that entrepreneurship is not easy. But I do believe that every lesson you have learned as an athlete has more than prepared you for the challenges.

As a business coach to many entrepreneurs, I'll give you my three keys to entrepreneurship.

Key number one is to find something that you are passionate about, something that you would love to do, whether you are making money or not.

Key number two, it must serve a purpose. If your business is something that you are passionate about and something that serves a purpose, it's more likely that you will survive all of the ups and downs of being a business owner.

Key number three is a big one. Profit! When deciding to pursue an entrepreneurial journey, it has to be something that will be profitable. And I repeat, it has to be profitable.

So, if we recap on my three keys, here is the summary: Find something that you are passionate about, that serves a purpose, and can be profitable. That is the best combination when it comes to entrepreneurship.

There is just as much risk in working for someone else as there is in entrepreneurship, but most people would disagree with that statement, and I can see why. I've always been more of a risk-taker, which is why entrepreneurship has always been my focus.

But if we look at the numbers, you can see why parents, friends, and mentors may not be excited if you decide to take the entrepreneurial splash into business. As I am talking to a committed athlete, my goal is not to detour you from being an entrepreneur. I'm simply laying out the pros and cons, so you can make an informed decision and be prepared for the challenge.

According to 2024 data from the U.S. Bureau of Labor Statistics (BLS), small business failure rates are as follows:

20.4% fail within the first year

49% fail within five years

65.3% fail within ten years[1]

---

[1] Commerce Institute, "What Percentage of Businesses Fail Each Year? (2025 Data)," Commerce Institute, March 27, 2025, https://www.commerceinstitute.com/business-failure-rate/.

The most common reasons for failure include lack of market demand, cash flow problems, poor management, and competition. So if entrepreneurship is your goal, you have to lock in and make it successful.

By actively pursuing the strategies in this chapter, you can position yourself for a successful transition into a career, graduate studies, or entrepreneurial ventures after sports. Even if this was not the most exciting chapter for you, I know that it will be the most important in the long run.

Continue to focus on maximizing your athletic career, but don't forget that you will spend more time not playing sports than you do playing, even if you make it to the league.

# THE BEGINNING OF THE REAL WORK

You've made it to the final chapter of *D1 Offers: Student-Athlete & Parents' Guide to an Athletic Scholarship*, but this is just the beginning of your journey. Reading this book was a critical first step—one that sets you apart from the countless others who are relying on hope, hearsay, or hype. Now it's time to take everything you've learned and do the work.

Throughout these pages, you've gained insight into the recruiting process, the mindset of college coaches, how to market yourself, and how to avoid the common traps that derail promising athletes.

But knowledge without action won't get you that scholarship. It's the daily effort, the willingness to show up when it's hard, and the ability to stay focused when no one's watching that will determine your success.

*For athletes:*

Your dream of competing at the Division I level is real—and it's possible—but dreams without discipline are just wishes. Every rep matters—every email, every highlight reel, every study session. You are building your future one small decision at a time. Stay coachable, stay hungry, and stay humble. You may be talented, but it's your work ethic that will separate you.

*For parents:*

Your role in this process is just as vital. You're not just a support system, you're a guide, an advocate, and sometimes the steady hand when your athlete faces uncertainty. Be patient, stay informed, and keep the long-term goal in mind: not just a scholarship, but a young adult who is prepared for the demands of college athletics and life beyond sports.

Rejection, setbacks, and challenges are part of the journey. Not every email will get a reply. Not every showcase will lead to offers. But remember: Your student-athlete only needs one coach to say yes. One program where the fit is right. So keep supporting. Keep refining. Keep believing—even when it's tough.

Here's a final thought: There's no shortcut to a Division I offer. But with purpose, persistence, and the right plan, you can turn the dream into a reality. Let this book be the launchpad, not the finish line. Your story is still being written—and the next chapter is yours to create.

Now go earn it.

# TURN KNOWLEDGE INTO ACTION

By now, you should have a clear understanding of what it takes to secure a Division I athletic scholarship. But understanding alone won't get you there—execution will. This is your moment to shift from reading to doing, from planning to producing.

To wrap up, here are five essential steps you should take immediately to move your recruiting journey forward:

**1. Evaluate your progress.**

Take an honest look at where you stand in the recruiting process right now. Are you on coaches' radars? Have you built an "entertaining" highlight reel? Do you know which schools are a good fit for your skill level? Identify both your strengths and your gaps, and make a plan to close them.

**2. Build & execute your recruiting plan.**

Don't wait for opportunities to come to you. Start reaching out to coaches. Register for exposure camps and showcases. Use social media strategically to highlight your talent, personality, and work ethic. Every message you send, every video you post, and every game you play is a chance to make an impression.

## 3. Stay disciplined—on the field and in the classroom.

A D1 athlete isn't just physically gifted; they're also mentally prepared and academically eligible. Your GPA, test scores, and study habits matter just as much as your performance. Train like a D1 athlete and study like a student who expects to compete at the highest level.

## 4. Expand and strengthen your network.

Surround yourself with people who elevate you. Connect with coaches, trainers, mentors, and former athletes who can share insight, vouch for your character, or open doors you can't open alone. Relationships are a powerful part of recruiting—build them with intention.

## 5. Be resilient and adaptable.

The recruiting process isn't a straight path. Coaches will come and go. Plans will shift. Injuries, delays, and disappointments will come. But if you stay focused, flexible, and unshakable in your belief, the right opportunity will come. Stay ready, so you never have to get ready.

# IT'S TIME TO EXECUTE

What is the difference between an athlete who hopes for a Division I scholarship and one who earns it? Execution. You've got the blueprint. You've got the knowledge. You've even got the edge most athletes never develop. But none of it matters unless you act.

Your future is in your hands. So keep grinding. Stay focused. Believe bigger. Then back it up with relentless action.

Need help getting started?

If the recruiting process still feels overwhelming or you just want some expert help creating a personalized plan, I've got you covered. I'm offering a free recruiting consultation where we'll break down your goals, assess where you are, and map out a custom Recruiting Game Plan to get you moving in the right direction.

Visit **www.phase1sports.com/d1offers** to schedule your session.

Let's take that next step—together.

See you at the next level.

*Mike Waters, Founder, Phase 1 Elite*

# ACKNOWLEDGMENTS

First and foremost, I want to thank God for providing the vision, strength, and purpose to write this book and carry out the mission of helping student-athletes reach their full potential.

To my family—your love, support, and patience have been my foundation through every step of this journey. Thank you for believing in me and standing by my side as I've pursued this calling.

To the entire Phase 1 Sports team—past and present—thank you for your dedication, passion, and commitment to the athletes we serve. This book is a reflection of the work we've done together over the last 20 years. Your contributions have changed lives, and I'm grateful to be part of a team that puts purpose before profit.

To the athletes and families who trusted Phase 1 with their dreams— thank you. Your stories, sacrifices, and successes inspired every page of this book. I wrote *D1 Offers* with you in mind.

To the coaches, trainers, mentors, and educators who pour into young athletes every day—you are the real superheroes. Your influence goes far beyond the field or court.

Lastly, to every parent and student-athlete reading this book: thank you for taking this journey with me. May the knowledge you gain here open doors, create opportunities, and lead you to the scholarship—and the future—you deserve.

# ABOUT THE AUTHOR

Michael Waters is a nationally recognized expert in student-athlete development, recruiting, and NIL management. As the founder of Phase 1 Sports, he has dedicated over 20 years to mentoring and guiding athletes toward their academic and athletic goals. His programs have helped hundreds of student-athletes earn full-ride scholarships and succeed at the collegiate level and beyond.

With a deep understanding of what college coaches are looking for and the steps families must take to navigate the recruiting process, Michael brings unmatched experience and passion to this industry. His mission is to empower student-athletes and their parents with the knowledge, strategies, and mindset needed to earn a Division I scholarship—and to thrive once they get there.

Michael is a sought-after speaker, coach, and mentor who continues to make a lasting impact on the lives of young athletes across the country.

www.ingramcontent.com/pod-product-compliance
Lightning Source LLC
Chambersburg PA
CBHW060439130626
46555CB00005B/2419